Not Forever in Green Pastures

Hugh Barnes -Yallowley

Photographs courtesy of my family, the Honourable Artillery Company and the Worshipful Company of Carpenters.

Front Cover painting from 'FIRLE BEACON' by Hugh Barnes-Yallowley

ISBN-13: 9781981128709
Published by Hugh Barnes-Yallowley

Thoughts for our Times

The encouragement received from family, friends and a former vicar of Berwick have led to the decision to publish personal poems written between World War 11 and the Millennium.

They have some historical significance as well as views on faith and the human condition. The poems can all be found throughout this volume.

Father, hear the prayer we offer:
Not for ease that prayer shall be,
But for strength, that we may ever
Live our lives courageously.

Not for ever in green pastures
Do we ask our way to be;
But the steep and rugged pathway
May we tread rejoicingly.

Be our strength in hours of weakness,
In our wanderings be our guide;
Through endeavour, failure, danger
Saviour, be thou at our side.

(Father, Hear the Prayer We Offer - Author: Love M. Whitcomb Willis 1859)

This book is dedicated to my wonderful children and grandchildren

Contents

Index of Poems

Introduction

"How it happened, Alice never knew, but exactly as she came to the last peg, she was gone. Whether she vanished into the air, or whether she ran quickly into the wood...there was no way of guessing, but she was gone, and Alice began to remember that she was a Pawn, and that it would soon be time for her to move."

Alice through the looking glass - Lewis Carroll

I am one of the lucky ones...... When asked to describe my earliest memory, it is not sitting in my pram or playing with my teddy bear, being dunked in a font by an overzealous priest or even having tapioca pudding shoved into my mouth by a nanny – I have a proper memory. It was being told that I was going to have a sister - even though I was only four and it was 1932, I remember feeling that this was pretty important news!......But let's rewind a little bit.

It has always been customary to begin a biography with a philosophical observation, designed to give the reader a quick flash of insight into what makes the author tick. Or perhaps to impress with one's philosophical knowledge...... I shall spare you all of that - for the moment!

My story does not begin at the beginning, because I belong to that peculiar generation whose views, upbringing and outlook were not forged by just one world war. As I was born in 1928, my generation is the one which links those pre-technology days of my parents, through the post-war austerity of the 1950s, culminating in the 21st-century iPad generation of the present day.

In many ways, as the song says we are all hostage to our parents hopes and fears and although we like to think that we spend a lot of our time rebelling and trying to distance ourselves from what we see as the foibles and deficits of our own parents, we eventually find that no matter which path we choose, and no matter how far that path is supposed to take us away from our parents, eventually we do become quite like them.

Why should that be the case? I really do believe that we are born with some form of inherited pre-programming which has a large element of predestination hardcoded into it, which means that coupling it to our upbringing and the set of attitudes that we inherit from our family, we may well end up following a similar path to our antecedents.

For instance, when my own father was born in 1894, Queen Victoria was still on the throne and I clearly recall him telling me that in 1909, at the age of 13, he wrote a school essay on Bleriot's first flight across the English Channel!

Only five years later he was in France fighting for King and country and even to the day he died, I don't believe that he ever fully understood how or why he survived those appalling days at Mons and the Somme. Just to reinforce how long ago all this took place, he used to recall that unbelievably he travelled to war with his own horse Queenie carrying a sword. He was shot in the leg and later in the war blown up by a shell – but survived to enjoy a very successful career and family life.

He fought with his two brothers, Arthur and Hugh (my namesake) – and Hugh was awarded the Military Cross, but unfortunately was killed by mortar soon after.

It was for this reason, because of the tragedy, that my grandfather forbade his remaining sons to marry while on active service. I fully understand what my father and his fiancée (my mother) subsequently decided to do, because it is exactly the sort of thing that I would have done. They eloped and married in a registry office in Rye - just before he returned to France in 1918.

No doubt, my grandfather was not amused, probably because he was a very serious man, which is exactly what you would expect of an actuary in the City of London. And speaking of predestination, he also believed that the City was really the only suitable place for his sons to carve out a career – and that is of course exactly what happened - not only to my father, but that is where my own career began and finished.

To many, I suppose, my grandfather was a rather foreboding man, but my memories of him are in very bright technicolour and entirely affectionate.

For instance, I clearly remember magically happy Christmases at his home, Clift House at Theydon Bois. My memories of that house as a small child were of a huge mansion with a glamorously imposing sweeping staircase with enormous pictures on the walls and lots of people everywhere. But then again, those are my Christmas memories.

We thought that Father Christmas would come out of Epping Forest, over the fence and through the garden... and we used to wonder whether we would meet him when we went walking in the forest. When we saw a deer Grandpa used to wonder loudly whether that was perhaps one of Father Christmas' reindeer. He certainly knew how to fire our imaginations.

I clearly remember the porch with its marble floor where we gathered on Sunday mornings, before we all trooped off to church. They say that the sense of smell is the most nostalgic of all the senses so that is why I presume I can still recall that slightly antiseptic smell in Grandpas porch.

There was one magic door leading from the porch to the main drawing room, which at that time was definitely the most magical room in the house because that was always the scene of Father Christmas' arrival on Christmas Day afternoon.

There was a morning room at the front of the house with an array of bell pulls which summoned the servants and there was a large safe door where Grandpa kept all sorts of mysterious objects - but mostly cigars, I think. What young boy would not have been impressed by a safe door within a private house?

The long dining room was across the hall where we all gathered for morning prayers every day.

Fairweather was Grandpa's valet and he used to bring the morning tea after having laid out all of Grandpa's clothes. I particularly remember Fairweather from the days that I used to go and stay with Grandpa and sleep next to him in his own big bedroom. I can tell you that it was both an awe-inspiring and (to a young boy) a very exciting experience to be plunged into such an exciting alien world. Grandpa would tell me magical things about the stars, the movements of the heavens, physics and geography.

Grandpa had a carpentry shop in the loft and I remember one day we went up there and made a small aeroplane out of a cigar box. Believe it or not, I eventually acquired that very work bench and had it installed in *my* home when we were at Gibraltar Farm many years later.

One of the great discoveries at my grandparents' home was the seemingly psychic way that Granny would summon people to the dining room exactly when she needed them. She would say something along the lines of *"The plates need to be cleared"* and, hey presto, as if by magic, someone would arrive to clear the plates. I found that *so* impressive.....until one afternoon, I slipped into the room on my own, searched around and found the cunningly concealed bell push under the carpet by her chair!

There is no rhyme nor reason for remembering particular events or objects from one's childhood and I presume that the ones we do remember are the truly remarkable ones. For instance, I particularly remember the way the hot water for the tea was kept hot by small spirit stove on the table. I have absolutely no idea why I remember that but it was probably because I had never seen such high-tech equipment before!

I also remember drinks being served to all the adults at Christmas time and Grandpa asking Fairweather in a very loud stage whisper*: "I wonder if we have any ginger beer for master Hugh?"* That was so exciting! Needless to say, Fairweather joined in the well worn dialogue*: "I'm not sure, but I shall go and have a look!"* After more consultation and of course great anxiety on my part, he disappeared for a while and inevitably returned with my ginger beer.

My great and continuing interest in art and specifically painting may have been fired by Millais' painting of Ophelia. You know the one where she appears to be drowning and casting flowers upon the water. A reproduction of the painting hung on the wall at the top of Grandpa and Grandma's stairs and it always used to terrify me because I wasn't sure what it meant but I could see that it was bad and sad. It affected me greatly, and obviously Millais' genius had succeeded in engendering the feeling within me, even though I was so young and could not really appreciate the subtleties within the painting or its 'back-story'.

Of course, the star room was the playroom with its fort and soldiers. Grandpa always kept them for me to play with and to enjoy but I was still very upset that I could not take them home with me.

To this day, I am very much involved in the church and even in my retirement do as much as I can to raise much-needed funds for our local church here in Firle.

Occasionally I wonder whether another memory from my grandfather's house continues to influence me. The playroom had not only a fort and soldiers but also contained a beautiful white cardboard model of a church. I have often wondered what might have happened to that.

Upstairs there was a very long corridor which, on occasions seemed to stretch on for ever. Grandpa's room was on the right and another mystery which eventually yielded its secret to me was his private cupboard. This is one of those little mysteries which fascinate a boy not yet ten.....children often wonder what lies behind a closed-door and that is probably why so many children's stories begin with a door!

Well, imagine my surprise when, after being sworn to secrecy I was shown Grandpa's Masonic regalia. Needless to say, I didn't fully understand the implication or what it was all about. But I do remember admiring the sheer glamour of the immaculate bits and pieces that I was privileged to share.

Unsurprisingly, a child's most vivid thoughts are about shiny things and sunshine. They are the ones which always seem to be the most deeply etched in the psyche. I am no different.

I recall playing on the lawn with my cousins from Liverpool, Thea, Angela and Elaine. My own sister Sara was a bit too young at that time to join in but I clearly remember how tiny she was.

When we children were ushered off to bed for the grown-ups to enjoy themselves downstairs, I remember laying awake and gazing out of the bedroom window towards the field opposite and wondering what the adults were up to. Whatever it was, it sounded like a lot of fun!

Memories of my grandfather are still very powerful. They are the memories of a very happy child who was not only in awe of but loved his grandfather very much and I feel sure that in his own passive, but very clever way, he did leave me not only with very happy memories, but, unknown to me at the time, a massive influence on what was to come.

These recollections of him are only one or two pieces in my life's jigsaw, but nevertheless I do feel that they are an important, integral and crucial part of what I became and what I am now.

I should mention, of course, that these were my father's parents, but my mother's side of the family was no less interesting and my maternal grandfather, who I remember as "Funny Gramp" is remembered as a real old character!

My maternal grandfather was well-known in Kent. He was a very successful timber merchant and in fact owned docks in Faversham. He was both a timber producer and timber importer, as well as owning several interesting properties, including a sweetshop, where I was delighted to be allowed to take my pick for free!

I recall Funny Gramps always taking my mother to Ascot and I also clearly recall trips to London theatres - and I seem to remember visits to the Strand Palace Hotel. Happy days! One of the stranger things I remember was his always (or so it seemed to me!) carrying what looked like a large wad of the old white £5 notes wherever he went. I suppose he was what might be termed a bit of an eccentric – but a very generous one!

Trips to the theatre were often punctuated by Funny Gramps disappearing occasionally and we naturally assumed that he had gone to the Gents...but later on I discovered that he'd in fact been speaking to his stockbroker. He was well-off and was a major shareholder in the now defunct Kentish coalfields. That particular investment was particularly appropriate for him as a timber trader because he was able to supply the mines with wood for pitprops etc.

The Barnes-Yallowley name crops up in all sorts of surprising places – and *much* more of that later – but equally interesting are some of the family's ancestral connections.

For instance, my grandmother (my father's mother) was a Harman. The Harmans have enjoyed an important and colourful presence in British life, and apart from owning a jewellery shop in Bond Street, several Harmans went on to distinguish themselves in British political life....the most recent of which is Harriet Harman, who carries on the family's Labour traditions. Harriet's aunt was Elizabeth Pakenham, Countess of Longford, and her cousins include writer Lady Antonia Fraser. Harriet is also a great-

great niece of Joseph Chamberlain. You may also be interested to know that an earlier Harman was a clerk to King Henry VII!

Our family has therefore been there and its entire history was documented in great detail in a family history which my father completed about 30 years ago.

As I've said above, my family link extends to the Longford family, which of course includes author and historian Lady Antonia Fraser. You may recall her father, Lord Longford distinguishing himself not only as a Labour peer, but as 'Lord Porn' when he headed up the pornography enquiry of the early 60s which led to those very radical changes in the United Kingdom's obscenity laws.

My father was definitely an 'analytical', as was his father. So it is very nice for me to know that at least part of my family has a creative and expressive side and throughout my whole life I have found a strange tension between my professional work, which was very conventional and analytical and my private life which I have to admit tended towards that part of my character bequeathed to me by my more artistically-minded ancestors.

Hence this volume is punctuated with the poetry that I have written from a very young age and which serves to remind me much better than prose or paintings of the various landmarks in my long life.

Of Death, and Life

When all was white with frost,
And Yuletide had come'
The Lord called
And he came
For his Earth's work was done.

In cloak of silent night,
With air cold and chill'
A man was
Born to Live
As Jesus said we will.

Thus weep not for the dead
But for the living cry
The dead Live
Leaving us,
The living still to die.

December 1944

Beginnings

At the age of five I probably wanted to be a train driver, although I don't clearly remember, but I do remember that I was very keen on trains and that we had trains at home, or should I say train sets.

I also remember always being surrounded by books. Even now, if you walk into my home, your first impression will be books. There are books on shelves, books on surfaces, books up the stairs, books above the doors, books in bedrooms, books in the dining room. In fact, for as long as I remember, I haven't stopped reading.

Between 1933 and 1936, I was at St Davids prep school in Purley. The school was just down the road from our house and my recollections are of being extremely happy and contented. I suspect that it was as early as my prep school days that I developed a great interest in drawing and painting because it is one of those hobbies that has stayed with me all of my life and which I continue to develop even to this day.

I decided not to cheat by trying to research the names of some of the teachers from those days, but I do remember one in particular. Mr Sutcliffe was my Maths teacher and headmaster at Downside School and I suspect was instrumental in developing the analytical within me! Strangely enough

I also recall details which nowadays seem anachronistic but then were the norm - and it is that teachers wore gowns!

A friend of mine at Downside was John Aspinall , who I met again several years later when we were both up at Cambridge and as I recall, our girlfriends were very close friends.

I remember battered wooden desks and even inkwells and dip pens, which I'm sure anyone under the age of 60 reading this will have no idea what I'm talking about. But let's just say that we did not have the pleasure of ballpoint pens, which hadn't yet been invented, nor even Fountain pens which were the exclusive domain of teachers and well-off parents!

Needless to say, as was the norm in those days, one of my major extra-curricular activities was being a Boy Scout – which was great fun!

One of the great changes to have taken root over recent years is that sports of any kind have taken second place to academic activities. So when I tell you that we had sports every single day and that the school had its own swimming pool, you will be able to see that we were a very fit bunch of children!

The other thing that I feel I ought to mention which seems so terribly Dickensian to the oversensitive folk of today, is the fact that corporal punishment was still available to all pupils, although as far as I recall, I did not take advantage of the service!

My sister Sara is four years younger than me and although I'm sure that we did used to play together, my memories are very sketchy and don't actually begin to mature until the age of about eight years old, and there's a reason for that. Much of British History is written around our Royal Family, so consequently, many of our collective memories are punctuated and brought to the fore by Royal events.

I remember 1936 and the excitement centred around George V's silver jubilee and just like children who were at school in the early 50s and who vividly recall the death of George VI and the subsequent Coronation of Queen Elizabeth, I remember one of my school assignments being a drawing of Buckingham Palace as part of the schools celebration of George V's jubilee. I especially remember that particular drawing because my mother had it hanging on her bedroom wall for many years.

At the age of nine, I was present and in fact played what I thought was a very important role at the 1937 HAC presentation on the occasion of its 300th anniversary. It was such a memorable experience that I have described it later in the chapter entitled the Honourable Artillery Company, where the family connection remains to this day.

In those days, my father had a Morris car and one of my sunny memories of those days was again when I was about eight or nine and I remember a trip to the Great Park at Windsor. You may consider that as a pretty pedestrian sort of memory, but in those days we would often go for family car rides - it was a tradition which continued well into the 1960s and 1970s – until driving a car became a chore rather than a rare treat.

What was different about this particular trip was that as we were driving through Windsor Great Park, there was a small open-top car in front of us. It contained George VI, the Queen, as well as their daughters, Princesses Elizabeth and Margaret! They waved and we were all very thrilled but I do reflect how times have changed. Imagine Queen Elizabeth and her family driving through Windsor Great Park today with no escort or security! Although I'm not 100% certain of the date, I do know that it was pre-war and that it must have been post-King Edward VIII's abdication.

I know that the King's abdication was in December 1936. As a result of the general population, as well as the political establishment being unwilling to accept Wallis Simpson as Edward's consort, his brother George acceded to the throne on 12 May 1937. That means that our very memorable trip through Windsor Great Park must have been either during the summer of 1938, or possibly 1939.

In any event, as you can possibly imagine, I was a bit of a hero when I returned to school and told everyone who cared to listen about my 'near contact' with royalty. The best my friends could muster was having seen the Royal family, maybe in a photograph or possibly on Pathe News - and here was I, the only person in my school actually to have *seen* the Royal family in the flesh and exchanged waves!

I was about eight or nine when I first remember people talking about the possibility of another war and I clearly remember hearing either talk or headlines of someone called Adolf Hitler and his invasion of the Sudetenland and then of course his assault on Austria, Czechoslovakia and Poland. There was a lot of discussion about the bombing that the Nazis had inflicted during the Spanish Civil War. But as children, we didn't really understand what was about to happen, although we had obviously heard about the horrors of World War I because most of our parents had been directly involved.

Is Every Bee attracted by Scent?

All things must grow old,
Of this is my story told;
For I'm sorry for the trees,
The Trees who still bear leaves,
But now the leaves of ivy
Or some other parasitic plant.

As the tree grows old,
The ivy takes her hold;
She becomes a cov'ring mass,
Without which he must crash,
But if the truth be told
His soul has already crashed.

She sucks his sap away,
She is come forever to stay,
For now he cannot resist
As she can always insist;
And when his soul is gone,
She'll live in a saprophytic way.

December 1944

My next memory was during what must have been called the Phony War, immortalised by the wonderful Dad's Army and although I had no direct contact or memory of the home guard, my best friend Michael Crook and I decided to be a little bit proactive and prepare for the coming invasion.

That takes me straight back to a book which I still own entitled *'A 1000 things for a Bright Boy to do'*. This book belongs to a genre which didn't die out until the mid-60s and which contained the sorts of ideas and experiments which would make a modern-day Health and Safety Inspector's hair curl.

Explosives, stink bombs, magic tricks..... this book was full of them. Nowadays, mere ownership of such a volume would probably result in a visit from the police or terrorist squad! Michael's parents totally forbade any of the potentially lethal and poisonous experiments to be conducted at his house, so consequently all the danger was transferred to my own home, but luckily apart from the odd minor accident, we survived.

Remember, we were both aged about ten, so we did not really understand our own limitations because at that age a child does not have limitations. The Daily Mail had recently published plans on how to make a shelter. Presumably, the assumption was that any impending conflict would be very similar in nature to World War I, so there were plenty of experts on hand to give tips, not only how to build a shelter but on how to mitigate against the gas attack and even how to deal with non-friendly parachutists.

Michael and I collected dozens of orange boxes which were about 2 ft.² and 6 feet long and we began to dig a large hole in my father's vegetable garden. The spoil from the hole in the ground was used to fill the orange boxes which we arranged one across and two on either side, arranged into layers so that very soon we had four walls of a shelter upon which we placed corrugated iron sheets which were weighed down with turf.

"To build castles in the air is to make a fool's paradise"

O to look upon the highest peak
Where the snow lies cool,
Still to look for distant lands
And to be a fool!
O to be a fool and seek
For a land unknown,
O to look on starry heights
And a golden throne.
O to live in ecstasy,
And to dream one's dreams
O to see the golden age
And to live, ... it seems, ..
As the happiest man alive
Without a worry or care –
But the happiest man alive
Has always a load to bear;
For thro' work he's reached his goal
And not be wishing long
For the joy he hopes to have
And the "World of Song"
"The World of Song" that in the eyes
Of those who see aright
Is far from coming while men seek
In the dead of night –
Without the sense to turn to God
The "One Almighty Light"

March 1945

Michael then pointed out, quite reasonably, that we should also be prepared for a gas attack because it was a time when gas masks were beginning to be issued. Consequently, one of my mother's best blankets was fixed across the entrance to our shelter with a bucket of water standing near to hand, so that in case of a gas attack, we could soak the blankets and that would give as protection against whatever gas the Hun decided to attack us with! We were ready!

We had even thought of how to deal with those enemy parachutists who would soon be raining out of the sky. We dug a large moat around the shelter and filled it with broken glass.

Needless to say, my father was absolutely livid and beside himself until we explained what we were trying to achieve. His rather brutal experiences during the First World War motivated him to construct a proper shelter for the family. It was in the lawn, made of concrete with metal reinforcement rods with a concrete roof below 2 feet of lawn. It had beds for four people and toilets. It was a work of art which made us feel really secure.

An additional deterrent was my father's First World War Colt 45 pistol, which would have been far more effective against those Nazi parachutists than our glass-filled moat.

We were not the only ones who took extreme precautions against what we imagined to be an impending invasion, which would no doubt be preceded by bombing raids.

I should remind you, that at the time we were living in Purley and I remember one day sitting in the garden with my family looking at the very first colour photographs that I had ever seen. In fact nowadays, I suppose you'd call them slides because you had to hold them up in front of you in order to let the light shine through. As Sara and my parents were busying themselves looking into the photos, we spotted something very sinister heading in the general direction of Croydon airport.

"London's lonely, as the country's homely"

As a leaf, I wander lone
Blown by an autumn breeze,
Blown along the cold grey stone
Of a city street, I freeze.
I freeze for the lack of a friend
The lack of a firm handshake
I feel as though my way I wend
Adrift on an unknown lake.
I am alone, yet in mass,
Of leaves of varied tints,
Alone like some poor country lass
In th'house of a might prince.
Thus, I wandered in a crowd
Of hurrying, scurrying men;
Talking, jostling, noisy and loud
And looking now and then
At a man here or a girl there
With merely a passing glance
Each concern'd with his own affair
And his business life of Chance.
"Can "cars" make friends with me
Or the statue in the square,
Or the Thames, which rolls to th' sea,
Or Wandsworth's commons' fair?
Of City! – how I hate you,
You only stand and stare ...
Have mercy when you view
This poor lone mortal's share."

Now, as a leaf I wander lone,
Or do I tell a lie?
The varied tints now seem to tone
And wind speaks with a sigh;
Here all the world is friendly
In this quaint old village place,
And folks they smile cheerfully
On a strange or unknown face.
They pass the time of day

These yeomen of this land
They guide you on your way
With Christian shake of hand.
Then out upon the highways,
Where few folks seem to pass
'Good morrow friend' the robin says
As he hops across the grass.
The country's friendly in a way
No artist can explain
The sweet perfume of new mown hay
The warm refreshing rain;
The measureless sky of azure hue
Sailed by countless clouds
Billowing sails an ocean of blue
With flapping wispy shrouds.
The stooks of kindly corn
Nodding their heads as they stand,
Glowing red gold at the dawn
Precious fruits of the land.
The chattering friendly brook
Talking all night and day,
Filling each cranny and hook
And gurgling on its way ...
Thus nature proves to me
Its friendliness to man;
Since God has made it free
To aid his mighty plan.

April 1945

What seemed like a massive number of aircraft were humming across the sky heading east and within seconds the explosions started.

Bombs were exploding in and around the airport and the local scent factory suffered several direct hits which resulted in a huge pall of smoke being visible for miles around. It was at that point that we probably realised that this was it!

What really brought the horrible harsh reality into sharp focus was one of the returning raiders dropping a bomb on Purley, quite near to our house.

In the excitement we had forgotten all about our shelter and all rushed round to see what had happened. It was a sight that I still haven't forgotten, probably because even now it seems counter-intuitive that a house should be devastated with one side of it having fallen away completely and yet with the intact staircase still standing. I still don't entirely understand the physics of it, but a staircase left standing after a house was devastated was to become quite a common sight in and around London.

The ubiquitous air-raid Siren still gives me the urge to run or jump into a ditch, whenever I hear one at demonstrations. In the Greater London area the first warning of trouble was very often a shower of spent machine gun cases falling from the sky as RAF fighters engaged the German raiders.

So the sequence of events would often be: shower of bullet cases, sight of aeroplanes, siren, run! On several occasions when I was cycling to school, I would hear the siren, leap into a ditch and be showered with spent ammunition cases.

Although there was little in Purley of interest to our Nazi friends, my father decided that it would be in the family's best interests to move away from London. Unfortunately, the choice of Milford on Sea was not the very best destination because it was in the general vicinity of the Portsmouth docks which eventually did become of interest to the Nazis.

We then moved to the Isle of Wight, which unfortunately was near the Solent, which was obviously also of great interest to Herr Hitler – we had an aunt there, but our stay was comparatively short.

Soon after our brief sojourn in the Isle of Wight, we moved to Bournemouth, and lived in a flat. I do remember listening to an orchestra in the park at Bournemouth and also my mother shopping. It is so difficult to imagine why one retains certain memories and rejects others, but I do remember walking with my mother and listening to a trio playing music in the street. I particularly remember a small combo playing piano and ukelele and it was about this time that I was first aware of music which then led me to buy my very first record – I don't recall what it was but I do know that it was a classical piece.

Although I was about ten at the time, I do remember that I was still wearing short trousers, as we all did in those days up to the age of about thirteen.

I seem to recall that after our Bournemouth flat, we stayed with an aunt in Northampton and what I do remember about her was that she was one of the very first lady doctors in England and her husband was a South African vicar and the Baptist equivalent of a Bishop.

Obviously wishing to confirm that there was *no* safe place anywhere in the British Isles, we then moved to various other areas, notably Northampton, where unfortunately we had to spend most of our nights in the cellar as the Luftwaffe bombed Coventry, just down the road.

Eagle House school in Northampton brings back mixed memories as I believe it was my very first discovery of the efficacy of corporal punishment and also remember my mother going to see the headmaster as the result of whatever misdemeanour it was, which had prompted my punishment. In spite of the bombing, we stayed there for one year and I recall making lots of friends.

Eventually, however, things quietened down a little bit in London, so we returned to Purley..... just in time for the second part of the Blitz.

The fact that so many houses were bombed, but staircases remained intact, gave the Minister of Home Security, Herbert Morrison, some inspiration because he developed an indoor shelter called the Morrison table. It was only an extension of what people were already doing because those who did not have a shelter dug into their garden tended to make small beds under the stairs because they realised that this was probably the safest part of their house.

The Morrison table was a very straightforward construction and as the name suggests, it consisted of no more than four steel uprights roughly the height of a normal dining table over which there was a steel plate with steel mesh around the sides, going from leg to leg. The steel mesh would give protection against any flying shrapnel, the steel plate would prevent debris falling on one's head, and its position under the stairs was the safest known part of the house, based on the empirical evidence provided by numerous Nazi bombing sorties.

In spite of its very simple construction, the Morrison table is credited with saving many lives and preventing many from being injured or maimed.

An Anderson shelter, a Morrison table or indeed anything short of a concrete bunker with 3 foot steel reinforced walls would have saved us from any direct hit - and we knew it!

However, most people who were injured, even killed, were not through direct hits but through shrapnel flying around after a bomb explosion. Nevertheless, as a small child, explosions and the whistling of the bombs prior to impact was pretty frightening. It also either tests, creates or consolidates one's faith.

Here's what my mother used to quote to us - and I have to admit that it did cheer us up, no matter how many times we heard it:

You will not fear the terror of the night.
Nor the arrow that flies by day,
Nor the pestilence that stalks in darkness.
Nor the destruction that wastes at noonday
A thousand may fall at your side,
Ten thousand at your right hand, but it will not come near you.

It is from Psalm 91 and I still find it very evocative.

For me, thinking about whistling bombs in Purley was soon to come to an end. I was about to be sent to boarding school in Huntingdonshire......and it proved to be one of the greatest early influences on my life and to a very large extent it also confirmed and gave me a massive impetus in my life's future direction – not only through what I learned but more importantly through who I met.

Kimbolton

"A mind not to be changed by place or time.
The mind is its own place, and in itself
Can make a heav'n of hell, a hell of heav'n."

John Milton, Paradise Lost

It was 1940 when I went to Kimbolton School as a boarder, and in spite of the fact that I missed my parents terribly, as is very often the case, I soon settled down to a routine and stability which I hadn't enjoyed with all the various moves prior to settling into this main part of my wartime education.

I refer to it as a wartime education because it was a mixture of both intellectual pursuits, divinity, as well as a lot of physical work – both sporting and agricultural – which in retrospect, I feel very privileged to have been exposed to and obviously pleased I did it because of the way that my career developed – but more of that later!

The headmaster of Kimbolton School was William Ingram, who was a fearsome character, although much loved by the staff as well as pupils. Mr Ingram had been at the school for many years and it was he who set the drumbeat for both the moral and intellectual development of all his charges. I remember him with much fondness and even corresponded with him when I went up to Cambridge, just after the war.

Inevitably, many of my memories of that time are not of the academic variety. For instance, I remember picking potatoes as well as the old-fashioned harvests, which was so much the highlight of the agricultural year and it was probably the very first time that I became aware of what can be achieved through teamwork. 'Stooking' wheat and barley before building

35

a haystack are terms you no longer hear but I am so pleased that I caught the end of what had been an agricultural method which had been used for hundreds of years. In case you're wondering, stooking used to consist of arranging sheaves of wheat or barley into wigwam-type shapes and arranging them in such a way in a field so that the wind would blow through them in order to dry them thoroughly before haystacking.

School dinners are another memory and of course those small bottles of milk (a third of a pint as I recall) which we would warm on the radiators during wintertime – I remember slightly warmed milk had a special taste all of its own. As you know there was a great shortage of meat during the war years, so occasional treats of bacon are well remembered, as are the occasional treats of tea, bread and jam.

One of the most welcome facilities which Kimbolton School enjoyed, and I hesitate to call it a facility but you have to remember that I was approaching my teens – was a local private girls school just outside Kimbolton – and I still recall the frisson of excitement as we walked into the village and saw girls(!).

The school was split into houses as was the custom until very recently. My house was called Ashfield house and there were 20 or 30 of us living there.

Toast suppers, tapioca pudding with rosehip syrup are all deeply ingrained in my mind, plus one other activity, (which I have to admit that although I learned how to do it, as it was part of my education, and have not made much use of since those days), was snaring rabbits and selling them locally – mostly to villagers. Remember there was a meat shortage!

Although we were all very well aware of the fact that World War II was in full swing at that time, I have to admit that we did appear to be living in a bit of a bubble because all the horrors of the war were not altogether clear to us until after it was all over. But you have to remember, those were the days before television and instant media and the only news would have been via newspapers and radio, which we did not particularly have access to. Perhaps that was just as well! However, we knew how to make a crystal diode radio and I was no different!

When I went to Kimbolton, incendiary bombs rained down on the city of London. British armies had been chased out of Norway and France but on the plus side, the Royal Air Force had established superiority over the Luftwaffe which they would never wholly lose during the entire war.

1940 was also a time when Britain acquired a new prime minister – Winston Churchill. I also recall what we used to refer to as the miracle of Dunkirk when 300,000 men were rescued from the north coast of France by what can only be described as inspired improvisation. Obviously, in those days, the full extent of the heroics of Dunkirk were not apparent to us but the one thing we were aware of was the fact that at that time an ill-equipped Britain had to prepare for what in those days was to be a very likely German invasion.

Earlier I briefly mentioned our headmaster, William Ingram. I am proud and privileged to say that I was a pupil during his tenure and in fact he retired just one year after I had left the school, having been headmaster since 1912. If I tell you he was born in 1887, you may have an idea of his rather complex set of views and attitudes. Nevertheless, it was under Ingram's stewardship that Kimbolton School became the educational force that it became and still is, to this day.

Until the day he arrived at the school, Huntingdonshire Local Authority was actively considering the school's closure.

When Ingram arrived in September 1912, he saw a rusting school crest in the entrance hall, bearing the motto 'Spes Duram Avorum'. He was both saddened and inspired because he felt that something was speaking to him – he saw the rusting motto as a cry for help. There was nothing dynamic about the motto of a school which appeared to be neglected, with an indifferent air among the incumbent headmaster Gosset Bibby and his staff.

Translated to English, this moribund establishment's motto, was *'May the hope of our forefathers endure'*. It was at that moment Ingram claims, that he decided to give himself *'mind, heart and soul'* to Kimbolton.....and he did.

Gossett Bibby was given two terms notice and handed over the keeping of the accounts to Ingram. It was 1913 and Ingram was still only 26.

He was interviewed on 28 March 1913 – one of over 100 applicants for the job of headteacher. The rest, as they say, is history.

When Ingram took over there were fewer than 50 pupils. In 15 years time, by 1928, there were already well over 200 as Ingram put his evangelical Welsh 'chapel' fervour to his work.

The changes which he initiated and embedded into Kimbolton School are far too numerous to mention, but by the time I joined in 1940, he had been at the helm for 27 years and the school was unrecognisable from the establishment he inherited in 1913.

It is also worth mentioning that not only was Ingram's superhuman effort evident in the Phoenix-like rise of Kimbolton School, but he was greatly handicapped by the fact that in 1922, his wife had died in childbirth so not only did he have to cope with the constant expansion of the school, but he also had to bring up three young children. I am also pleased to report that the schools old boys Association – the Old Kimboltonians continues to go from strength to strength.

Incidentally, we were affected by World War II in as much as there was a certain amount of disruption by blackouts being put up on all the windows, all torches being confiscated and part of the playing fields being converted into a kitchen garden.

Air raid shelters were erected and sandbags were filled by pupils. It was certainly hands to the pumps.

I remember that at the time school numbers were approximately 300, and remained so for the duration of the war.

One massive blow to Ingram was the 1944 Education Act by which education authorities were given the responsibility to secure *'an adequate provision of primary and secondary education'* and tuition fees and maintained schools were forbidden.

A bombshell was delivered to the school governors in 1944 when a spokesman for the Hunts CC Education Committee stated quite uncompromisingly:

"We have considered our scheme for education for this county as required for submission to the Ministry of Education and I must inform

you, gentlemen, that in our plan we can find no place for Kimbolton School"

This was shattering news for Ingram, especially in light of all that he had achieved at Kimbolton. He had hoped that Kimbolton could have been designated a state or county boarding school – but the local education authority was firm and started to use Kimbolton as the boys Grammar School for the St Neots district.

Ingram was left with little choice - apart from either going totally independent or applying to the Ministry of Education for the status of a direct grant school. Ingram was not very keen on the independent route and as there was a war it was very unlikely that an independent school could have been launched at that time.

There were indeed many bureaucratic obstacles to reassigning a school to be directly funded by the government, notably because one of the rules stated that any school applying to be a direct grant school would have to be in possession of a substantial endowment of its own.

Ingram knew that the school's original endowment had been sold off, mostly well before he had joined the school, so being the creative thinker he was, he turned to the school's old boys.

The response from the old boys was immediate and exceedingly generous with the consequence that Kimbolton School became one of only four schools to be given direct grant status.

Of course, my contemporaries and I were not aware of the maelstrom of politics that Ingram was involved in during our stay and it is indeed a measure of the man that we remained blissfully unaware of the stress and uncertainty that he had been subjected to.

He finally retired in 1947 and in the title of his own autobiography he alluded to what he felt was his bequest, that is to say, what his life's work had created at Kimbolton. The book was entitled *'The Power in a School'*.
I have taken a little bit of time describing William Ingram because I really do believe that he was an influence on me in so many ways. He was driven by that rapidly dissipating mixture of discipline, competence and what can only be described accurately as religious conviction, from which he drew both strength and which drove his moral compass.

I have never forgotten him......, not least for the fact that he was very instrumental and part-architect of my next educational move.

It would be very remiss of me not to mention one other very important aspect of my life, which remains important to me. Kimbolton School was the place where I first became interested in sailing and in fact I was about twelve or thirteen, when I learned to sail a boat.

I remember sailing around the Norfolk Broads in the days before they looked like a boat housing estate and I even remember the name of the boat I sailed. She was called ERALITE and I remember her well.

I could not even dream that 10 years later, in 1950, I would be crewing in the Camper Nicholson yacht LUTINE – owned by Lloyd's of London.... But before then, there was a lot more water to flow under my personal bridge.

The Meteor

Men toiled
Horses stirred
The bridle rattled its tune,

Th' ploughshare cut
The soil turned
The sun was at its noon …

Autumn waited
The leaves fell
The shafts of the sun grew dim

A 'plane roared
The earth shuddered
The smoke was as black as sin …

A funeral pyre
Of white hot heat
Labourers rushed to the spot

Fire bells clanged
Sirens shrieked
But the flames they noticed not.

Sunset came
A sky of blood
The guard with bayonets stood

For 'neath the turf
A mortal lay,
At least, his mortal hood …

The dawn rose
On misty heights
The wreck lay, bare, forlorn.

Men lived;
But o'er the sea
Some women now will mourn.

Kimbolton
November 1945

Called up?

"Sometimes it is the people no one can imagine anything of who do the things no one can imagine."

Alan Turing

It was 1946, the war was over and surely the British government would have no use for someone like me - but I was wrong! National service beckoned!

It was all very sudden. There was a letter which required me to report to Padgate. I had never heard of Padgate - probably because it was somewhere near Liverpool.

I don't particularly remember the train ride, but I do remember once I'd arrived being asked to put all my civilian clothes in a bag and being shown some films about all sorts of things with which I was not familiar – including, shall we say, some well-known ailments which are not normally the subject of after-dinner conversation!

If I'd been given a choice, I'd prefer to have joined the Navy, but as I'd been in the ATC during my time at Kimbolton, the British army's opinion was as follows:

" You have Highers in Maths, etc, so you're the ideal candidate for looking after RAF radar"..........Military Logic!

How could they possibly have known or even cared that during my time in the ATC I had flown with the RAF. It was only in an old De Haviland

Rapide biplane, but nevertheless I had flown . Plus, I had also flown as Waist Gunner in an American Airforce B17 Flying Fortress....but that certainly did not mean that I was either interested in or knew anything about radar.

And so began eight weeks of basic training, during which we were taught all the skills needed in order to survive as an airman.

On that first night, we were handed our kit which appeared to consist of old serge WW2 ex-army uniforms which had the texture and comfort of grade 80% emery board. In fact, we were given two identical uniforms with one for everyday use and the other for parades.

We were ordered to report to the cookhouse, so we grabbed our mess tins and trotted off for our first military meal. In spite of the fact that we were making allowances for the fact that there had just been a war on and rationing was still very present, I can confidently say that I was just about to experience one of the worst meals of my life, eaten in a prison-like atmosphere, under the hawk-like gaze of a duty corporal or sergeant (I didn't look up much) who you felt was just waiting for you to pull a face or complain about the stuff that had been thrown into our mess tins and which only bore a passing resemblance to food. It was vile.

I sighed quietly to myself as I realised that in all likelihood the grey substance in my mess tin would probably be the staple diet for the duration of my stay in the services. I also remember lots of shouting.
Did I distinguish myself during my very short pre-university military career? Well, I can claim that I was very much involved during the Berlin airlift, when I was seconded to the Headquarters of 46 group somewhere north of Watford.

We were underground, and unfortunately the radar content of my work there was practically non-existent. We were corresponding with air traffic control who were organising the flights in and out of Gatow, Berlin and I vividly remember the incessant clattering of teleprinters as various codes and bits of information were transmitted to our department.

The Berlin Airlift took place from May 1948 until May 1949 when the Soviets lifted their blockade. However, flights continued right throughout the summer of 1949 and ended in September. The very last plane into Berlin was the same as the first – a DC Dakota. It bore a message on its nose from Psalm 21: *For they intended evil against thee; they imagined a mischievous device, which they were not able to perform.*

Although we carried out our work below ground, we were billeted in cabins above the ground and the only point of real interest that I would like to recount is that my future wife's uncle (and it would be nearly ten years before I even knew of Anne's existence) was Chief Air Marshall, who then went on to be a DC to Lord Mountbatten and ended up as Britain's most senior officer in the Far East.

He'd also been shot down at Dunkirk, rescued from the Channel and resumed his flying almost immediately and went on to serve with Douglas Bader in Tangmere, in Bader's Spitfire Squadron.
When my time at HQ 46 group came to an end and I was demobbed, I came back to Cambridge and was asked to go and see Claude Guillebaud , who was to become my tutor at St John's and a kind friend.

My memory of that initial meeting is sketchy, but it was a pre-enrolment meeting and I remember we talked about political economy.

Here is a poem about flight which I have always found so inspiring and which reminds me of my very first flight:

"Oh! I have slipped the surly bonds of earth,
And danced the skies on laughter-silvered wings;
Sunward I've climbed, and joined the tumbling mirth
Of sun-split clouds, --and done a hundred things
You have not dreamed of --Wheeled and soared and swung
High in the sunlit silence. Hov'ring there
I've chased the shouting wind along, and flung
My eager craft through footless halls of air...
Up, up the long, delirious, burning blue
I've topped the wind-swept heights with easy grace
Where never lark or even eagle flew --
And, while with silent lifting mind I've trod
The high untrespassed sanctity of space,
Put out my hand, and touched the face of God."

'High Flight - John Gillespie Magee Jr

Cambridge

"I wish life was not so short.......Languages take such a time, and so do all the things one wants to know about"

J. R. R. Tolkien

I have never been an intellectual and had I imagined even for one moment that I was gifted in any special way, that would have been totally dispelled by some of the people I met over the next three or so years during my university days.

The Cambridge of the late 1940s was still very much as you might imagine it might been had you read Brideshead Revisited!

I was fortunate enough to attend St John's College, Cambridge, which was founded in 1511 and when you think that it was established as a result of the express wishes of Lady Margaret Beaufort, who happened to be mother of Henry VII, you can imagine that when you walk into those beautiful buildings, you can almost taste the history.

The town of Cambridge is all about the University. There is a general feeling that most of the town's population comprises either of students or those engaged in various support functions designed to develop within it a certain intellect and code of behaviour which would form the basis of everything they did when they finally graduated. Every single Cambridge graduate takes away not only a Masters degree but certain 'je ne sais quois' which distinguishes Cambridge graduates from graduates of other all other universities – including Oxford!

The MA (Cantab) also means that you can become a vicar but as I was only tempted very briefly, I report that fact purely as a Cambridge anomaly!

Peterhouse was founded in 1284, and so is Cambridge's earliest college, whereas Jesus Christ's and St John's as their names may suggest were created as a result of the dissolution of small religious houses and establishments. St John's had been the Augustinian Hospital of St John up until the early 16th century. In fact, the college's original accommodation, First Court, was built between 1511 and 1520.

The St John's original chapel dating from 1280, was incorporated into the new college and over the next 500 years various additions were made to the college, culminating in the Fisher building designed by Peter Boston, which was completed and commissioned in 1987.

In the very early days, a typical student would have been between 13 and 14 years of age and the Morning Bell would have been rung at 4 a.m – something which I suspect would be potentially fatal to the modern student!

Nevertheless, scholars of one sort or another were already up at Cambridge in the early 13th century, providing income for the towns landlords, but it didn't take very long for houses to be hired by the various colleges as student hostels with a Master in charge of each set of students.

The importance of Cambridge as a centre for learning was realised as early as the reign of Henry III, when he became aware of the fact that Cambridge students were being overcharged and generally badly treated by commercially minded Cambridge citizens.

King Henry took the scholars under his protection in 1231 and not only arranged for them to be protected from exploitation, but also granted several privileges, some of which remain to this day. For instance, one of the very important ones to impoverished undergraduates is the fact that colleges can sell beers, wines and spirits without having to follow normal licensing laws – and all at a very advantageous price!

When I arrived in 1948, there were approximately 8000 students scattered among the 23 colleges and although we all considered ourselves as Cambridge University undergraduates, one's first loyalty was always to one's college. In my case it was as a Johnian – and believe it or not, that feeling continues to this day.

Some of the royal privileges conferred by Henry III were considered generous by certain people and so on arrival at college, undergraduates had to be officially enrolled for purposes of identification in order to establish their rights as an undergraduate. This so-called matriculation, in other words, a presence on the Masters roll, (otherwise known as a *matricula*) is de rigueur, and even to this day a student is not identified by his year of graduation but by his year of matriculation.

When I arrived in 1948, St John's undergraduate matricula stood at about 600.

It is always very tempting to regale readers with lists of distinguished Johnians and my initial intention was to only share the names of my contemporaries who went on to do great things, but St John's College has produced a dazzling array of scientists, mathematicians, economists, businessmen and even five prime ministers, so I'm sure you will forgive me if I briefly indulge myself and share with you a very brief list – just to give you an idea of the eclectic mix of graduates who went on to distinguish themselves.

England cricket captain Mike Brearley, photographer Cecil Beaton, as well as author Douglas Adams already hinted at the variety of students who have passed through the hallowed halls..... And of course, let's not forget actors such as Derek Jacobi and one of the early exponents of British satire, Jonathan Miller – who cut his show business teeth as a member of Cambridge's Footlight Review, together with Peter Cook, Dudley Moore and Alan Bennett. Surprisingly, however, Derek Jacobi did absolutely no acting at Cambridge, although he was already involved with three or four external acting companies.

Needless to say, and in spite of my main subject (which I shall tell you about later) I became a very enthusiastic member of the Lady Margaret players.

Drama has always been a very important and strong part of the College's academic curriculum and a very important part of its ongoing entertainment. It was while I was up at Cambridge in 1949, that the Lady Margaret players was re-formed, in spite of the fact that the college lacked a suitable theatre... although there were some very successful summer outdoor productions.

The height of my own college acting career was in the piece, entitled 'An Evening in June'. A facsimile of the programme is reproduced in this volume on Page 86.

As Johnians, our strong traditions and achievements are best exemplified by the fact that both of Cambridge University's weekly student newspapers, Varsity, and the Cambridge Student were founded by Johnians, namely Harry Newman and Ien Cheng.

Still recognised as one of the great television series of all time, 'The Glittering Prizes', which was a series transmitted by the BBC in the 1970s, was written by Johnian, Frederic Raphael. He said himself that it was meant to update the image of the Cambridge student and was intended to put Brideshead Revisited *'In its place'*. Quite right too!

Rafael turned The Glittering Prizes into a novel which certainly captured the heady mix of blind ambition, competition and intense deep personal relationships which characterise modern undergraduate life in Cambridge. Or to be more accurate, Frederic Raphael was in fact reminiscing about his time at St John's College. In fact, if you look at the cover of the novel of the series, you will see Tom Conti, the star of the TV series sporting a Johnian scarf with St John's College buildings as a backdrop.

So how did I end up at St John's College, Cambridge, swimming in that pool of what I can only describe as 'extreme talent', some of whom are now household names?

I believe that I may have been placed at Kimbolton for strategic reasons, because there was a family tradition of attending St John's College, Cambridge and added to that Ingram knew one of the Fellows at St John's – R L Howland. For me, the circle was squared.

There was no big 'Hooha' about 'going up to Cambridge'. It was merely the natural continuation of an education - a straight through course. In fact, five Kimboltonians went to Cambridge that year.

My 'Highers' were French and Mathematics, so what I needed was a good generalist subject and at the time, it happened to be one which was comparatively new – Economics or to give my course its full name: Political Economy.

Yes, there had been economists around for a very long time but the topic had not been formalised to any great extent as a University subject. In fact, what I studied was Political Economics – which covered everything from the numbers, economic history, right down to a study of the unions. In fact, I thought, on balance, it was taught as a bit of a left-wing subject, but nevertheless I found it thoroughly interesting and enjoyable.
One of the highlights of my time there was a working trip to Ford in Dagenham to learn about mass production, as well as a visit to Italy to study the production of small Italian cars.

Lectures were mandatory and we all wore gowns to lectures and in the evenings.

Economics had been taught in Cambridge since the late 19th century but it was very much a Cinderella subject and was taught in those days as part of moral sciences and history Triposes and as late as 1910, there were only two students!

By the time I arrived in 1948 the economic tradition had been more or less established and my supervisor was C W Guillebaud who had been teaching at the college since the 1920s.

Many well-known economists have passed through St Johns, notably Mervyn King who was a teaching fellow in the early 70s. He obviously went on to become Governor of the Bank of England. Gavyn Davies was another graduate who went on to become not only economic adviser to 10 Downing Street but then went on to become managing director of Goldman Sachs and chairman of the BBC.

One of the great economists of all time, and one who I feel is very often overlooked is Alfred Marshall, who was also a Johnian. His 'Principles of Economics' was certainly the 'go to' economics textbook for a very long time. As a matter of interest, he was the uncle of my supervisor, Claude Gillebaud!

One of Marshall's students was one John Maynard Keynes – another Cambridge man and from what I understand, an enthusiastic member of the Bloomsbury Set!

I have mentioned Marshall, not because I ever came across him – he was far before my time, but because of his legacy at St John's. Marshall saw economics as 'an engine for the discovery of concrete truth'. He was interested in uncovering the causes of poverty and through rigorous quantitative analysis had a strong commitment to improve human welfare through influence on public policy.

It is said that his view has characterised many of the Johnian economists who followed – and I believe that to be true, even in my own case.

But it was not all work work work!

In spite of the fact that wartime rationing was in full swing, we were expected to dine at the college five times per week. The best thing that I can say about the food is that it was adequate. I have to admit, in spite of the fact that there were food shortages, and in spite of the fact that our diet was very limited, I have no recollection of it ever being an issue.

In my day, the Union was more than a debating society, handily situated adjacent to the Mitre pub, straight outside the College gates.....and although I never participated in any debates as a main speaker, I do recall how entertaining many of them were – you have to remember that in those days we literally did have to make our own entertainment, with most of it being in-house.

I particularly remember one debate, which had a guest speaker called Eamon de Valera of Ireland's Fianna Fáil. I remember his passion and erudition as he spoke of Ireland's crises. At the time, he was already President of the Council of Ireland and of course later, he went on to become President of Ireland. He was a very impressive character....and there is no modern Irish political history without de Valera – from being one of the commanders of the 1916 Easter Rising and finally his presidency.

In the future, I would become a member of the Common Council (more of that later) as well as a member of the Honourable Irish Society where we were very much involved in raising standards in both Northern Ireland and Eire.

The Union invited the whole spectrum of society to its debates and although I was deeply affected by de Valera's words, I wonder whether I would have been as impressed by one of the subsequent speakers, Marshal Tito of Yugoslavia, who apparently turned up, not looking so much as a head of state, but more like a Cinema commissionaire, with more medals and decorations than a Christmas tree.

I truly believe that I was lucky enough to be up at Cambridge during the Golden Years when so many young people on intellectual fire were still forming their ideas and I was privileged to meet some of them – among them Fred Hoyle who worked extensively with Coastal Radar with which I was involved during my National Service.

 Alan Turing was another brilliant mind I met– of course at that time we had no idea of his invaluable work on the German Enigma machine at Bletchley Park. Sadly Turing committed suicide in 1952 as a result of having been prosecuted and convicted of homosexual acts. It took the British government until 2009 to offer an apology and issue a full pardon.

Turing's mentor at St Johns had been Max Newman, who was a fellow between 1923 and 1945. Newman had been the head of the mathematical section at Bletchley Park. It was he who first had the idea and built Colossus, which was the first electronic digital computer used in code breaking. Newman is generally credited for having first encouraged Alan Turing to work on complex mathematical and statistical reasoning required for code breaking.

Dr Eric Match was a friend of Sir Maurice Wilkes. He introduced me to the Cavendish Laboratory and EDSAC (Electronic Delay Storage Automatic Calculator) which, in 1949, was an early British computer.

Another famous name at St John's was Professor Paul Dirac and his equation for the electron. Dramatically, this equation predicted the existence of anti-particles for the electron.

Sir Percy Craddock, who became ambassador to China (1978-1983) was another enthusiastic member of the Debating Society. I also recall Professor Harry Hinsley who was later knighted because of his work at Bletchley Park, which, as you might imagine at the time, was 'sub judice'.

Looking back, my most influential lecturer was Bertram Russell. Everybody crowded to his lectures. Some of them were so erudite that students could not keep up with him! It was at that time that I studied his famous book 'The History of Western Philosophy.'

I must not forget another great friend, George Guest, the organist. He produced a large volume of Johnian music which has been professionally recorded.

Quite apart from personalities in John's, I took a great interest in the picture of William Wilberforce in Hall because he was responsible for the abolition of the slave trade and I already knew that he was a close relation in the Barnes-Yallowley family at Clapham.

When I wrote my poems on John's, I was particularly impressed by Nashe's eulogy of the college:

'..... *that most famous and fortunate Nurse of all learning St John's in Cambridge, that at that time was a University within itself'*.

Yes, those glittering prizes! Even coming into contact with people who would go on to become much more than merely a footnote in history has a profound effect. I'm convinced that through a mysterious process of psychological osmosis, just coming into brief contact with such celestial intellects can have a deep effect on one's life.

But from the sublime to the ridiculous..... When I first arrived as a rather nervous and gauche undergraduate, there was no computerised allocation of timetables, digs or anything else. I was greeted at the door by a porter who had a photograph of me. His first question was *"Have you got a gown?"* – which I didn't – but very soon did. He kindly found an old gown for me – with the original FOUR stripes!

The St John's undergraduate gown is of the usual shape but without a forearm slit. Over the resulting forearm seam there are four black velvet bars. In Cambridge university slang, the velvet bars are referred to collectively as 'crackling', in reference to the nickname for the individual bars as 'hogs'.

Apparently once upon a time, students of St John's were referred to as *hogs*. Don't ask!

In those days all undergraduates wore gowns in public and colleges closed the gates well before midnight, which served well to teach many students (including myself) the art of scaling the wall after dark.

As far as lodgings were concerned, they consisted of a sitting room, small kitchen, a bathroom and a bedroom and it was traditional for all first-year students to live within the college, with second and third year students taking advantage of the many licensed lodgings within the town. I was one of the lucky ones and spent all three years in-hall.

As you probably know, the only accepted mode of travel for undergraduates in Cambridge was and continues to be the bicycle. In those days, bicycles were not the sleek, lightweight machines that we see nowadays. They tended to be rusting black heavyweight machines and if you ever found one with three Sturmey Archer gears which worked, you were indeed blessed.

In spite of the fact that the vast majority of the bikes were no more than a two wheeled heap of rust, they had to be registered and have a number painted on them.

Cambridge was very unusual in those days as the lectures took place in the morning and the afternoons were given over to more energetic activities as well as debating.

However, there was one activity, which was certainly not as high on our minds as perhaps it should have been – but that in itself is a debate.

Sexual activity in those days was very limited, unlike the apparent free for all we hear about these days. Yes, there were ladies' colleges: Girton and Newham....and there was also a teacher's training college (Homerton).

For the really desperate there was, of course, Addenbrooke's Hospital, with the senior nurses accommodation at Queen Anne's Terrace. This was certainly one area of the town which experienced quite a high undergraduate footfall and was (and probably still is!) known locally as QAT.

For most of us, there was the much more civilised tea dance at which we could be introduced to young ladies and to be quite honest, that is where most of us tended to practice our soon to be needed 'chatting up' technique to those equally inexperienced pink faced undergraduate ladies. In retrospect, it was all such innocent fun but then again, as I was quite useless at football and cricket, it was a cheap enough sport in which to involve oneself.

It was almost exclusively the fault of the, shall we say, extra-curricular activities involving the fairer sex, which caused some of us to commit the occasional transgression because we all had to deal with the rather vexing problem of the college doors being closed at 10 o'clock and then locked at 11 o'clock.

Logistically this caused many of us severe problems because pubs would shut at 10:30 p.m. so if one included the drinking up time, perhaps followed by a brief assignation with a lady friend, (which normally took at least 15 or 20 minutes), one's appearance on the tutor's Late Arrival Report was not unusual.

Fortunately, most transgressions were treated very fairly. But I do remember once being summoned by the Rev Canon J S Bazzant who was Dean of both Chapel and of college discipline. I remember him as quite a scary character with a bit of a reputation as a stickler for discipline. For instance, there was one occasion when he sent down 30 undergraduates on one day, but reprieved them the next.

One of the more famous stories about him was when an undergraduate was caught 'in flagrante' - probably scaling a wall and upon realising that he had been observed by the Rev Bazzant himself , he hissed *"Oh, God!"*. Quite unperturbed, Dean Bazzant simply observed *"Not God, just his earthly representative!"*. History does not record the fate of the hapless miscreant.

When I found myself in front of the Dean, after having scaled the college wall after hours, I still remember the trepidation with which I entered his office but luckily he was as charming and as understanding as could be, and simply said to me very pleasantly: *"What sort of sherry would you like?"*

He explained to me that life is about choices and all the choices I was making now and would make in the future were my own responsibility and whether I believed that my choice of scaling the St John's wall was a particularly good choice for me to have made.

I have never forgotten that particular encounter.

Unlike nowadays staying out late *was* a big issue. Written permission was required if one needed to be out after midnight. For instance, a theatre trip to London would mean taking the last train back, which was at 11:30 p.m. That would mean arrival at the college in the early hours of the morning. That further meant that there was absolutely no way that it was worth the risk, without obtaining that letter of authority.

However, if one was naïve enough to believe that staying out all night was the best way forward, that too was a very bad move. That was as a result of yet another well-established Cambridge tradition – that of the 'bedder'.

The bedder was retained by the college in order to enter one's room and make up the bed as well as generally tidying up. Unfortunately, bedders tended to be wives and daughters of porters who would feel bound to report any unmade bed to the appropriate authority.

Generally, one became very used to the rather benign 'cage' of college discipline because it was not particularly onerous (for those days) and one certainly learned that there was a price to pay for the privilege of being an undergraduate in such a glorious establishment.

I can also understand all these years later that the discipline imposed on undergraduates was not there for its own sake, but within it there were quite profound lessons about courteousness, thoughtfulness, as well as learning the great attribute of appropriate personal behaviour.

Speaking of appropriate behaviour, one of Cambridge's great institutions is The May Ball which rather interestingly is held in June. More precisely, I should say 'a' May Ball because all the senior Cambridge colleges held a ball which filled that awkward gap between those rather frenetic examination weeks and those much anticipated summer days when we all went down for the Summer Vacation.

I remember June as being not only a very expensive summer month but I suspect that it involved more physical activity than all the previous months put together. Not only did the May Ball have to be negotiated, but as a rower, I had the May Bumps rowing events to contend with. Needless to say, even the May bumps were in June. That's tradition for you!

The more affluent among us would 'drag' from one May Ball to another, dance, eat either side of midnight, then dance until dawn. A boat or (for the more energetic or sober) a punt would be hired and one would drift down the river for breakfast and then back to town for bed. In my first year (in Lady Margaret) a boat was burned outside New Court! Don't ask, but there was probably a perfectly rational explanation!

The St John's Ball was held in-hall, where every evening we used to eat our evening meals. In addition, there were several marquees for the overspill. For the May Ball the Hall would be transformed into a magical place as powerful lights would be placed outside the fabulous stained-glass windows and shone inwards, creating a magical atmosphere. Of course, it wasn't just hordes of undergraduates but the Master was there, as were the Fellows.

Dinner was served in the 200 foot long panelled Senior Common Room with a matchless atmosphere created by being lit by candlelight and with the tables distributed along the length of the room and covered with white linen tablecloths, which appeared to glow in the magical light.

You may be interested to know that it was traditional at St John's, and only on very special occasions, to serve *swan,* but records show that there has been no consumption of swan during the 20th century, although there is some indication that swan was served at Christmas dinner during the 19th century.

In spite of the fact that platters were adorned with a fake swan neck and wings we were probably eating chicken or rabbit!

For some reason, I am again reminded of Venice where my colleagues and I met two very nice American girls and I vaguely recall Venice's Bridge of Sighs, so-named by Lord Byron who fancied that as the bridge was the last Venetian view that convicts would enjoy before being incarcerated in the nearby prison, adjoining the Doge's Palace.

St John's College has its own Bridge of Sighs. It connects the Third Court and New Court. Its resemblance to the original Bridge of Sighs is a little tenuous as the only two common factors are the fact that it is also made of limestone and crosses water. Mind you, it does have windows which are sort of similar to those within the Venetian structure plus the fact that it is a covered bridge. In any event, I am firmly of the opinion that the bridge crossing the Cam is aesthetically *far* superior than the original bridge crossing Venice's Rio di Palazzo!

No account of anyone's undergraduate days would or should be complete without at least a passing mention of a pub or two. I was quite often to be found at The Eagle, which of course has now gone into legend, as a result of Watson and Crick's DNA announcement of 1953.

Whereas The Eagle was quite handy for the scientific community who even to this day busy themselves with the computations and experiments at the Cavendish laboratory, it was another pub called the Mitre which was much handier for us Johnians as it was straight across the road from the college.

I seem to recall lots of American accents in the pub – probably because it had been adopted by the Mildenhall Air Force Base with its contingent of American airmen.

One of the guiding lights throughout my undergraduate years was my tutor Claude Guillebaud. He was one of the colleges 'solid citizens' and had in fact been a teaching Fellow since the 1920s. If you find his name vaguely familiar, it is probably from the quite well known Guillebaud report of 1956, where he had been commissioned by the government of the day. The report was entitled 'The Enquiry into the Costs of the National Health Service'. Just that title suggests that in the intervening 60 years, little has changed.

The enquiry had been called by the then health Minister Iain Macleod and Guillebaud had been Macleod's tutor at Cambridge.

Guillebaud went on to write several standard economic textbooks, so I feel very privileged at having had the pleasure of him being my tutor during my time at St John's.

I was at Cambridge from 1948 to 1950 when, as I mentioned before, rationing was still in full swing and I'm perfectly aware of the fact that at the time many people in the United Kingdom were not terribly well off so it may surprise you to hear that during my student days, I took my very first holiday abroad with two friends. Although these days, it all sounds a bit pedestrian, we took a train ride to Trieste – which in those days used to be in Yugoslavia. It is not generally known but Trieste had been partitioned in a similar way to Berlin, so it was always important to make sure that one was on the correct train platform.

We visited Opatilo, which I can only describe as being as similar to Monte Carlo as you could possibly have imagined. We also made a very memorable trip to a small island called RAB. There we met up with some very attractive French girls and had ample opportunity to practice, amongst other things, our spoken French.

Another trip I took, which I think was probably in 1950 was to Venice, where not only did we meet two very nice American girls, but I had my very first experience of boating on one of those shiny varnished Italian speedboats called Rivas which seemed so glamorous at the time and which you can still see in those in old James Bond films.

So I can claim to have travelled in a Riva, which incidentally is the Rolls-Royce of speedboats....and all by the time I was still in my early 20s. I thought that was quite an achievement!

It would be very remiss of me if I didn't mention Daphne. One of my great interests has always been singing and I seem to recall that Daphne was a really excellent singer and believe it or not, much to the consternation of her parents, I asked Daphne to marry me.

I am not sure whether they couldn't, at that time, visualise my excellent prospects but nevertheless we were properly engaged and Daphne (for a while) wore my ring. Unfortunately, just like many of these early engagements, this one fizzled out as both Daphne and I became involved with other people – no doubt to the relief of Daphne's parents and my parents.

Throughout my Cambridge days, I shared lodgings with my friend Brian Wills who became a very dear friend.

Before we wrap up this particular section on my rather exciting undergraduate life – incidentally, I *did* graduate and I'm still very happy to see MA (Cantab) after my name –I would just like to mention two of the rather important people that I met as an undergraduate. Both are as different as they could possibly be but both contributed greatly to the world in general. In very different ways.

I knew Fred Hoyle socially, but I don't recall whether he'd actually formulated his Big Bang Theory by then because I seem to recall that even as late as the 1960s there were two distinct camps of physicists: the Big Bang people and the Steady State people. As we all know now, Fred was the Big Bang man and that is now the generally accepted theory of the very beginning of the universe - and I have actually met and dined with him! As my grandchildren might say – *"How cool is that!"*

Finally, there was Brian Cartledge. Brian is three years younger than me but we were contemporaries at St John's and became friends and in fact we remain friends to this day. As I went off to pursue a modest career in the city (more of that later),he took a double first in history and went on to become one of our more distinguished diplomats, having served all over the world including Russia at a very crucial time in its history. He even went on to become an adviser and PS to both Margaret Thatcher and James Callaghan, as a result of his unmatched overseas affairs expertise

Finally, there was one person who was consigned to legend, very early in his life and that was Francis Crick, who gave his legend that initial colour by announcing his discovery at the Eagle pub in Cambridge. I was not present, but I do recall several people thinking that his pub outburst sounded like the idle boast of a drunk! That is until either the following day or the day after, when the headlines appeared indicating that two men named Crick and Watson had discovered something called DNA.

So, as you can see just based on some of the people that I have told you about, I was truly blessed by having been up at Cambridge at such a vibrant and exciting time.

The Big Wide World

"Try not to become a man of success, but rather try to become a man of value."

Albert Einstein

I don't particularly remember any post-graduation traumas and although I was not yet clear exactly what I would be doing with myself for the next few years – after all, I was an economist - I did manage to ease myself into what would become a lifelong career in the city with some help from my family.

Meanwhile, please allow me to digress for a paragraph or two. It is worth mentioning (my thoughts of Daphne reminded me) that I am a lifelong opera fan and for a large part of my life I have made sure that I'm not more than a few miles away from Glyndebourne and its very famous opera house.

The Glyndebourne Festival Opera has been held since 1934 and I know the present owner Gus Christie, but I clearly recall that I was at the Edinburgh Festival in 1950 – soon after my graduation – and at that time I had not yet been to Glyndebourne, because it had not yet developed into its present form.

However, many years later I was having a conversation with Gus' father, Sir George Christie who was the son of the festival founder John Christie – and he too had been present at the same Edinburgh Festival! That may not seem all that unusual now, but you have to remember that in 1950, the festival was new and nowhere near as popular and crowded as it is now.

We both thought that was rather interesting coincidence!

I have called this section 'The Big Wide World' because it was time for me to launch my career and what was to become my great City adventure – and believe me, it was a fantastic adventure at a time when new post-war attitudes were seeping into every aspect of British life, and I was lucky enough to live through it all.

By far the greatest changes were within the City of London.

When I went to work for my uncle Cecil Barnes at his accountancy firm, those were still the days of no regulation, bowler hats, rolled umbrellas and "*my word is my bond*". It is hard to believe that within 40 years I would witness cataclysmic changes in both my personal and professional life.

Uncle Cecil had a small firm of accountants – as I recall only about fifteen people – and the office was near to the HAC building. My job? I became articled to my accountant uncle and completed the first two of the three articles by the time I left two years later.

Barnes, Dunn and Bowton was a traditional old accountancy firm – I still remember the dark mahogany and although the work for a junior such as myself was pretty mundane, I learned a great deal about auditing and double entry book-keeping as the firm had many professional clients. You have to remember that in those days there were no computers or even electronic calculators, so accountancy was very much about columns of figures within large ledgers. It was all very time-consuming and at times quite tedious – but I knew that it was something that I had to do and it helped me to understand proper business.

Remember that all of us had very strong memories of the war and in spite of still seeing damaged buildings and being subjected to food rationing, we were all full of enthusiasm and hope.

Just to demonstrate how much progress has been made since 1950 you may be interested to know that the 1950 general election was the very last one which was fought without the rather dubious benefit of television coverage. As history records, to everyone's surprise Clement Attlee slid back into Downing Street with a parliamentary majority of six.

Even five years after the end of World War II we were still so pleased to hear that the bacon ration was to be increased from 4 to 5 ounces a week and that ½ ounce was going to be added to the sweet ration! The interesting thing was that simultaneously the West German government announced the abolition of petrol rationing, as well as an end to all other rationing, apart from sugar.

Many wondered who in fact, had won the war!

I also recall Klaus Fuchs, who had been charged with communicating secrets to Russia and in America, Sen. Joseph McCarthy was busy purging communists...... And as if the Americans had not had enough of war, they were busying themselves in readiness for the Korean conflict.
So you can see that although things were pretty mundane in Britain, the world in general still had not settled down from the trauma of World War II.

Interestingly, meetings had already been held by European heads of state in order to discuss both the political as well as economic union of Europe. Although at the time this was no more than an interesting development, it certainly fuelled my interest for what I was to achieve in the future in what I can only describe for the moment as a pan-European insurance venture. But all that was still a few years in the future and would see me travelling all over Europe and eventually all over the world, constantly extending the influence of British finance and insurance expertise. More of that later!

Meanwhile, I do recall French General De Gaulle, who had been so badly treated by the Allied high command during World War II making his mark and, in the opinion of many, showing great foresight by telling the fledgling EEC (known as The Sic) what he thought of their European federalist fantasies. Remember that Britain had been persistently refusing invitations to join in. It took nearly twenty years for Britain to join the EEC, but by then I like to think that businesswise, I had already conquered Europe!

In 1952 I joined Alexander Howden's as a junior employee – as I recall the word 'clerk' was still in common use, and if you'll allow me to indulge myself just one minute I shall fast forward a number of years and tell you that I eventually became chairman of the group – but in the early 50s I was right at the very beginning of a long and winding road during which I would not only see my career develop, but witness the most cataclysmic events unfold within the city of London.

Some of you may have heard the name Alexander Howden and not always in the best possible light. But when I joined as a junior in 1952 it was a very successful but ordinary insurance broker.

Once again, it was a case of starting at the bottom as a clerk, carrying and delivering insurance slips and gradually getting to know my way round the city and specifically, Lloyds of London.

Needless to say, life was once again pretty mundane to start with. However, I was already formulating my ideas for the future which reminds me of a question I'm very often asked nowadays by those who know my career connections with Lloyds. They ask me

"You know your time in the City, what do you think was your greatest achievement?"

Was it the glamorous days I spent in Monte Carlo? Was it running with the 50s Chelsea art set? Was it meeting people such as Joan Littlewood or Lucien Freud? It was none of those.

My greatest achievement of the 1950s was meeting and marrying Anne.

Anne

The post-war years in Chelsea had a style and innocence which I don't think will ever be recaptured.

Although by nature I am most definitely an analytical, I have always had a great interest in the arts. Not just some of the arts, but all of the arts. I'm a poet and a painter and I adore opera and going way back to my pre-university days as a member of the Chipstead players. When I was living in Chelsea in the 1950s, the sort of people I gravitated towards were definitely the arty types.

The renowned producer with the Chipstead Players used to be Joan Littlewood and I think it was in 1953 when she opened her theatre workshop at the Theatre Royal in Stratford East – many years before the East End became fashionable and it was largely thanks to the social world that I had become involved in through my work colleagues and their rather interesting social lives that I met Anne.

At the time she was a very beautiful and demure young lady, but even then I could see the force of nature which she developed into and I have to say that everything that has happened in my life since those far-off days were made much easier with Anne by my side.

My first flat in Chelsea was in the block right next to Chelsea Town Hall, which is quite handy for the Kings Road and the coffee shops which were springing up all over the place. I stayed there with Colin Willmott who was a Johnian and an old Kimboltonian and he was noted for the fact that he married Shirley Eaton, the golden girl from the James Bond film 'Goldfinger'. Eventually, my friend Graham Gosney and I bought a flat in Hereford Square where we could fully exercise our not inconsiderable social life which happened to revolve round those theatrical types that seem to have invaded post-war Chelsea.

You may recall me mentioning SEESEAS, which was very much a social phenomenon which not only resulted in some very splendid dinner parties during my time in the RAF but had also saved me and other members of the club from some of the most onerous tasks which were being dished out, mainly thanks to a very paternalistic and friendly staff Sgt. I only mention that because the type of people that I tended to gravitate towards in the old SEESEAS days were exactly the sort of people that I was meeting in Chelsea and thanks to whom I met the love of my life.

As a keen theatregoer, I recall meeting Clement Freud at the Royal Court Theatre Club and then being invited to a party at Clement's brother Lucien's house, which was also in Chelsea but, if there *is* such a thing – at the rough end of Chelsea! That is where I met Anne.

At the time, my future wife Anne also shared a flat. She lived in Sloane Gardens and rather fortuitously she and her flatmate called 'Mossy' had also been invited the party.

I don't think she was particularly looking for any romantic complications because as I recall from a conversation she and I had, she was very much in love with someone else at the time and as I recall, I was also engaged to someone else.

I met Anne rather innocuously by starting to chat with her as I was tipping some wine into her glass. We very quickly established that we quite liked each other. We had quite a lot in common – the most bizarre coincidence I remember was that we both had rather bad car accidents in France.

We chatted for a long time, finding great rapport and then I suggested that we inspected the roulette as there was a table in full swing at the party. Anne was very successful at roulette and I think it may have been at that point when I decided that she was the sort of person that I should stay quite near to - and she was wearing clinging silver frock of the type in fashion and again, just what appeals to me.

But then Anne and I had both been engaged before and an engagement was quite a serious commitment because in those days it meant 'engaged to be married' rather than the current 'engaged' or 'going out together'!

Anne invited me to the flat she was sharing with Mossy and two other girls for breakfast next morning on the roof. I recall that the flat had access to some sort of rather dangerous roof terrace. She was wearing a pretty cotton dress just bought at Fenwicks and we all enjoyed sitting in the spring sunshine.

The Edenbridge point-to-point was quite an event as I would probably bump into quite a few of my university chums so I invited Anne to drive down with me in my green Ford Prefect and after a little bit of deliberation Anne agreed to come with me, although she was very conscious of the fact that she was still dressed for a party in Chelsea and therefore a little overdressed for a point-to-point in deepest Kent!

'Green Ford Prefect?', I hear you ask.... Yes, it had been my mother's car and I was very proud of it. I recall that I was the only person in the world who knew how to turn it on because I had become fed up with people breaking into it and being able to start it. Consequently, I'd had a battery immobiliser switch fitted in a secret location under the dashboard...., but I digress!

In spite of Anne sporting her happy cotton frock among all the sensible tweeds, we had a wonderful day and all ended up at the Spotted Dog in Edenbridge.

Anne suggested we drove back to Ditchling and I could spend the night there. I was whisked up to a flat upstairs - it wasn't in the house but above Anne's father's surgery.

It is rather difficult to be invited to someone's parents' house on a first date – and all that Anne would tell me when she brought me a glass of orange juice was not to say *anything* of any consequence to her parents!

I was introduced to Anne's mother and then we went up onto the Downs for a chat! We were definitely getting on very well! But then I was due for lunch at newly-wed Judy Scott-Barret.

I decided very early on that I was *very* interested in Anne and I had managed to obtain tickets for the hottest show in town which was 'My Fair Lady' coming over from America. Graham and I had two tickets each and neither of us had at that time decided who we wanted to take, but I think my short time with Anne had left me in no doubt. So, in spite of the fact that Anne wasn't too sure that she would be able to go with me, we went to one of the first showings of My Fair Lady in the West End.

At the time Anne was involved in the very glamorous advertising world. She was working for McCann Erickson, where she was involved in everything from the Nestle account to Picadilly cigarettes. Remember those?

In June, we went to Henley........ where else? Anne remembers that I wore my Lady Margaret blazer and I remember her looking ultra–chic in a white dress with polkadots, and a very small waist. Of course we went into the stewards enclosure because that *was* the place to go.

The social whirl continued and I took Anne to the HAC Summer ball where I believe she'd already assumed that I would propose to her – which I didn't.... probably through fear, but within a month I had asked Anne to marry me and she accepted!

I suspect that Anne had had quite a few proposals in her day and I am so pleased that she accepted mine.

It all happened so many years ago and we both remember it as if it was yesterday. My proposal was at the rather unromantically named Monkey Island in Bray, which at the time was run by Constance Spry and Prue Leith.

So there you have it, the greatest achievement of my early career – although when I proposed to dear Anne, I was already a Lloyds broker and am very happy to report that we are still together nearly sixty years later. I will tell you about our wedding, honeymoon and our later life together but I thought this would be a good time to introduce Anne.

My great-great-great Grandfather. Born 1753

St David's School

- FATHER -
- MOTHER - HUGH - GRANDPA
- SALLY -

Just before the war

Top: Kimbolton School

Bottom: A B17, Flying Fortress over Kimbolton….The very first plane I flew in.

Shades of Chariots of Fire! I was a sprinter! Won a cup for the Hundred Yard sprint.
Kimbolton 1944.
(I thought I could run until one day I was thrashed by Chris Brasher!)

Brian Corby was my friend - and I don't mean that in a trivial or casual way.

We first met before World War II, when we both attended Kimbolton School. Subsequently we both went up to St John's College, Cambridge where Brian read Mathematics and I read Economics. We both even completed our National service in the Royal Air Force!

Although our careers were roughly within the same sphere, I initially went to work for my family's Accountancy practice in the City while Brian joined the Prudential as an actuary. We both ended our careers as chairmen of various companies - with Brian having remained with the Prudential for his entire career and ultimately becoming its very distinguished Chairman.

Brian held several other high-profile posts, including Chairman of the Association of British Insurers as well as President of the National Institute of Economic and Social Research as well as several other important positions , including something which appealed to his fierce academic streak which was his appointment as the very first Chancellor of the University of Hertfordshire.

He was knighted in 1989 and became Sir Frederick Brian Corby - although to me he was always 'Brian' and I have to admit that I would never have completed my Maths Higher without Brian's help. Consequently, I always felt that I owed Brian a great deal.

His burgeoning intellect was already apparent when we were at Kimbolton - even as a schoolboy he would complete the Times Crossword before breakfast!

It was Brian I went to in the Eighties when, as a Lloyds Member and a Lloyds Brokerage Director, I shared with him my concerns about many of the business practices surrounding Lloyd's of London. (At the time. Brian was already a member of the court of the Bank of England).

Brian died only three years ago and although I miss his wise counsel - mostly, I continue to miss one of my closest friends.

My friend Brian Wills and I....Undergraduates in 1948.

Graduated. 1952. The Bridge of Sighs is in the background.

By permission of the Master and Fellows of St John's College, Cambridge. (Reference: SJCA/SJCS/28/2)

Same crew....but in the top photo, I'm on the right (in the bow) and in the 2nd photo, we're headed in the other direction! This time, I'm on the left!

Scholars Lawn

Proud Parents!

'The Chipstead Players 1956
(I'm the one standing in front of the window)

HQ 46 Group – Berlin Airlift.....It was good to have played a small part.

Sailing on LUTINE......Cowes 1958

Anne looking very relaxed!

At Xandra and Roger Frewen's wedding in 1959

Isles of Scilly 1964

A 1964 business trip to Holland – after Jane's birth

Preparing to move to Gibraltar in 1968.....with Caractacus.

Anne and I at the Old Beach Hotel, Monte Carlo in 1968.

A 1970s family unit!

With all the happy family at Gibraltar 1974.

Barnes-Yallowley Coat of Arms

(Joseph Barnes was the Master of the Paynter-Stainers Livery Company (1788-9). Hence the three shields embossed on our Coat of Arms.)

THE CARPENTERS' COMPANY

Broadsheet - March 1992

Introduction

This is the second Broadsheet to have been issued with the aim of informing the Livery and Freemen of the Company of various aspects of the Company's affairs and to update them on recent events. It is hoped that articles written in the Broadsheet will generate interest as a result of which there will be, perhaps, a greater participation in various aspects of the Company's affairs than has hitherto been the case. The Carpenters' Company is a living body and it can only thrive by the active participation of those who are privileged to be members - particularly of the Livery.

Message from the Master

The Company's first Broadsheet last October brought you up to date on activities in the City and the Company and how the Company is organised through the Court and its committees. Now is the time for the second Broadsheet and we have decided to concentrate on the craft aspect of the Company. Modern Liveries are all founded on specific trades and professions which are currently an important part of the City of London. The older Companies have, in a number of cases, lost their true craft activity and have had to concentrate on charitable matters related to the original craft. As Carpenters, right up to the Great Fire of London, we were the house builders and so we can be proud that over 40% of the Livery is still associated with the building craft in one way or another - builders, surveyors, architects - and still a few actively involved in carpentry itself. The Company therefore continues to be involved in assisting the craft and promoting excellence therein, as it has ever since our earliest records in 1271. Craft competitions, our Building Crafts Training School and representation on outside bodies by Liverymen account for a major part of our activities in addition to our principle in-house charities of Rustington Convalescent Home, Godalming Almshouses and Carpenters and Docklands Youth Centre at Stratford. This record of involvement by the Company will, we feel sure, make those Liverymen and Freemen as yet not involved, proud of the role played by our Livery Company.

The Master, Mr H M F Barnes-Yallowley with Mr M O P May, the President of the

The Worshipful Company of Carpenters
Carpenters' Hall
Throgmorton Avenue
London EC2N 2JJ

Here I am wearing my Common Council tie ! I served 1986-2000.

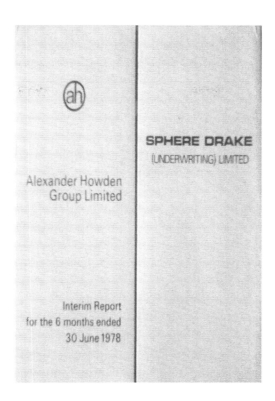

Above are two examples of literature belonging to many of the companies which I set up and was the Chairman of. Here are some of the others:

1964-77	Director	Alexander Howden Ltd
1970-78	Chairman	J Arpel & Company Ltd
1973-83	Managing Director	Community Reinsurance Corp Ltd
1974-78	Chairman	Solar Group Ltd
1978	Director	Alexander Howden Group Ltd
1984-86	Director	Lyon Group Ltd
1987-91	Director	Bennett Barnes (Underwriting Agencies) Ltd

Jonathan and Antonia's wedding. October 1987. Chapel, Royal Chelsea Barracks.

Welcomed at Highgrove in 2003........Was my gardening knowledge adequate?

I first met The Prince of Wales with Captain John Lippiett RN at the Tower of London in his ship HMS NORFOLK and two senior officers who knew my son Jonathan. We were only six people at lunch in the Captain's cabin in HMS NORFOLK and I explained to him about the Building Crafts College and said that we would welcome him if he became a Liveryman of Carpenters. I followed up with a letter and he became a LIveryman and inspected the college that day.

Relaxing….Master of Carpenters 1992

Welcoming Admiral John Lippiett, CB, CBE, DL at Carpenters Hall in 2016.

Memories of my trip and exciting times on HMS Norfolk

Enthroned!
Master of Carpenters 1991.

Three Barnes-Yallowley Grandsons

Portrait by Debs Gregson

Me with artist Debs Gregson - wife of Carpenters' Company Clerk, Brigadier Tim Gregson MBE.

The Dockland Settlements
Charity No. 306025

About Our Charity

Serving Dockland Communities since 1919

I have enjoyed working for this charity since 1955 – Interesting Clubs nationwide.

In the footsteps of
Uncle, Great Uncle and Great Great Uncle

Captain Hugh Cyril Barnes MC

2nd Bn Royal Sussex Regiment

~

A Family Pilgrimage and Tour
To
The Great War Battlefields of Loos, The Somme and the Ypres Salient
26th - 29th October 2006

~

Brothers **Arthur, Francis** and **Hugh Barnes** joined the Honourable Artillery Company (HAC) early in 1914. Many thought the war would only last a few months. They went with the first British Expeditionary Force (BEF) on the ship Westmeath and were immediately involved in the defence of Belgium. They took part in the Ypres battles and have stars on their medals to show they were there when the 'Angels of Mons' appeared. There were so many casualties in the early part of the war that the HAC became a officers cadre and were split up and were seconded to other regiments. **Arthur** became a Captain in the Somerset Light Infantry; **Francis** the 7th Bn Queens, known as The Buffs and **Hugh** into the Royal Sussex Regiment.

Arthur and **Francis** were wounded in the first part of the war; **Arthur** was shot in the head and **Francis** blown up. After treatment in France, they returned to Kent to train the continuing young recruits and then both returned to the front and took part in the major battles of the Somme. **Francis** has particular comments about Sanctuary Wood battles in Ypres. **Hugh** was decorated with an MC at the Battle of Nieuport 1917 and towards the end of the war, 21st July 1918, blown up when enemy shell exploded the Trench Mortar (TM) Ammunition dump during a raid by his own battalion. His memorial is at Loos Dud Corner Cemetery although he has no known grave.

~

Touring Together

Hugh and Anne Barnes Yallowley
Vivien Wolstenholme
Andrew and Carro Wolstenholme
Toby Barnes Yallowley
William Barnes Yallowley
Hugo Binney

Max Barnes Yallowley
Lottie Wolstenholme
Jonnie and Antonia Barnes Yallowley
Arthur Wolstenholme
Charlie Barnes Yallowley
Harold Wolstenholme

Eddie Barnes Yallowley

A moving and fascinating family trip to the great battlefields of ww1. Eddie was there and a wonderful member of the group.

Three generations of Barnes-Yallowleys remembering family members who took part in the Ypres battles.

77. *Building Crafts Training School, 1970: initially teaching all building crafts, the College now concentrates on woodworking and stonemasonry.*
◄

I am very proud of having been instrumental in the re-establishment of the Building Crafts College into the great success it is today.

A family picnic at Glyndebourne.

Al Fresco at West Place House

Off to Ascot!

Another family gathering in the Woodard Room at King's College, Taunton for Max's confirmation.

It's DEFINITELY in the blood!

Goodwood.

Springtime in Firle.

Captain Hugh and crew messing about on the river.

They DID say "Come as you are".......Firle Fireworks

Still going strong! Anne and I at the 2016 Charleston Festival. PROPER retirement!

ST PETER'S CHURCH, WEST FIRLE, EAST SUSSEX

REPAIR WORKS CARRIED OUT SINCE 1994

All costs are exclusive of VAT (* indicates date of faculty recommendation)

Re-roof south nave and Gage Chapel, remove boiler house & re-point flint work, repairs to gutters etc	1994*	
Replace window chancel south side clear glass	1997*	
Reroofing of south aisle	1999	£ 4472.00
Trial repair of south aisle ceiling	1999	£ 443.68
Redecoration of interior	2000	£13036.68
Misc repairs to windows	2000	£ 123.00
Redecoration of south porch	2001	£ 587.50
Repoint part of nave west wall and tower	2001	£ 2290.00
Purchase of new light fittings	2001	£ 3600.00
Relighting and wiring	2002/3	£ 9044.28
Sellwood tablet	2003/4	£ 123.50
Repairs to south aisle west window glass	2004	£ 1680.00
Repairs to south aisle west window masonry	2004	£ 2287.00
Reset gravestones etc	2004	£ 3987.00
Retile north aisle	2005	£ 8319.13
Repairs to south aisle windows and plinth	2006	£ 4800.00
Repairs to north aisle windows	2007	£ 1665.00
Bells	2006/7	£27541.00
Work to tower associated with bells	2007	£ 3697.00
Work to porch masonry and other masonry repairs	2009/10	£12057.00
Renovation of the West Tower**	2012/13	£83,285.00
Funds raised towards the North Extension**	2014/16	£67,000.00
		£250,038.77

** includes legacies totalling £75,000

Just some of the funding I have helped to raise locally over the last few years.

Alexander Howden

"My word is my bond"

"I know of men who believe in themselves more colossally than Napoleon and Caesar. I know where flames the fixed star of certainty and success. I can guide you to the thrones of the Supermen. The men who really believe in themselves are all in lunatic asylums."

GK Chesterton

If you were to look at my CV, Alexander Howden occupies a large part of it. Its footprint on my life is quite substantial.

I was very happy to have joined a Lloyds broker, especially one which was beginning to look outwards and spread its wings internationally. Make no mistake, Howden's gave me great opportunities to travel internationally. Much of it connected to large World Bank projects such as hydroelectric projects and dams, but more importantly my job was to build bridges between far off insurers and the London market.

Ultimately, there were sacrifices to be made, especially as when I accelerated my offshore travel my family was still very young. In fact I could be away for as much as three months of the year.

I worked in Argentina, Brazil, Japan, as well as Thailand, Australasia and Canada. The whole of Europe, especially Scandinavia were also on my itinerary.

My Christian belief has always played a large part in my life, even to this day. So I felt much like a missionary spreading the reputation of Britain, Lloyds and the stock exchange all over the world and in fact some of the places I visited had never been even contacted by someone from the city. Those were real ground-breaking days.

In addition, I felt that it was not all done *just* in the name of profit but that I was contributing positively to the welfare and well-being of people all over the world. For instance, the El Chocon project which provided hydraulic power to Buenos Aires or the Manglar Dam in India or the famous Kariba Dam in Africa were all part of my work.

Then, of course, I was involved in insuring the very first jumbo jets as well as being involved with oil rig problems.

Remember that we were still in the days of the Iron Curtain and the Cold War and I was very pleased to fly to Poland to discuss international reinsurance with the government, as well as Polish insurers. I can say hand on heart that I enabled the Polish economy by arranging international credit insurance in dollars and sterling so that they could buy equipment which they could not possibly buy with their own currency, the zloty.

Just to amplify how things were behind the Iron Curtain, I recall my host taking me to the opera and being surprised to find that almost the whole of the audience were Russian soldiers rather than Polish nationals.

I shall always remember one trip where I was flying back from Finland and found myself on a Russian plane with no one speaking English. I had the temerity to order a drink and a glass of water was produced, accompanied by a copy of the latest Russian five-year plan.

Those were the days which spanned the late 50s and early 60s, when I worked for a traditional company which enjoyed an excellent reputation and I had hoped that this difficult but uncomplicated way of doing business would continue forever. Unfortunately that was not to be..... and I shall tell you about that in some detail a little bit later because it is a very different phase of my business life to the one described above, and it is that change which was the catalyst for the seismic changes both at Lloyds and in the City and where I, unwittingly, found myself far too close for comfort to the epicentre.

By 1964, I was a director of Alexander Howden and by 1978 I was director of the Alexander Howden *Group* with various other chairmanships running contemporaneously. The intervening years had seen Alexander Howden flex its muscles and gradually acquire several well-known names before it too was bought by an American corporation – and even that became a bit of a scandal.

The Wedding and Beyond!

"Whatever our souls are made of, his and mine are the same."
(Wuthering Heights)

Unsurprisingly, the story of most of my life is also Anne's story and I will now pick it up at our Church of England wedding in Ditchling church.

Anne's parents were slightly daunting, her father was a psychiatrist and needless to say, Anne had warned me that her father would probably try to psychoanalyse me when we first met, but he and I both got on extremely well. My future father-in-law was in fact a GP who then went on to do some rather important neurological work at Hurstwood Park Hospital, near Haywards Heath and then at Roffey Park.

Here we were – me at the age of nearly 30 and Anne at the rather tender age of 22, very much in love and both very happy to cross into each others' worlds ....and I certainly had no issues in being introduced to Ditchling society!

We were married in Ditchling church on 10th September 1958. Both the setting and the guests made this an extremely British and romantic wedding and as a bonus it was Anne's uncle, Air Chief Marshal Sir Hector McGregor who proposed our health.

It doesn't seem so long ago, but when I tell you that the popular music charts were being controlled by Connie Francis, Dean Martin and the Everly Brothers, you can see that our marriage preceded the modern pop scene by several years!

I didn't tell Anne where we were going on honeymoon. We spent the actual wedding night at the place where she'd accepted my proposal two months earlier – Monkey Island in Bray.

We flew to Naples and I clearly recall when we landed poor Anne being terribly embarrassed when a young man arrived with a huge bunch of red roses from my company's Rome office. We both also remember the unnecessarily speedy drive along the coast road by a driver, whose proud friend announced as a rally driver! We hoped knew the road *very* well, especially as we were not keen on the opportunity to examine the sheer drops as we sped along the coast.

We stayed at the 'Pensioni Holiday' in Positano which is what nowadays would be called a 'bijou' hotel. It was all very romantic and we had a very lovely time. It was a small place but a potter down downhill took us to the Bucca de Bacco where I introduced Anne to Italian liqueurs in the moonlight watching the sea.

At the end of the fortnight I was asked to go into my company's office in Rome, which not only gave us both a foretaste of what life was to become and how inextricably linked it would be to my work, but it was also a wonderful surprise for Anne when we were booked into the Hotel Eden in Rome.

This five-star hotel on the Via Ludovisi is not only a spectacular building but is also very handy for everything from the Coliseum to St Peter's Basilica. Although (if the truth be told) sightseeing was not the number one item on our agenda, we did spend a lot of time getting to know Rome at its most romantic.....and there's nothing more romantic than Rome viewed through the eyes of a honeymoon couple!

Anne's mother had helped to put her trousseau together but she yearned for Italian shoes (!) and although out for a good couple of hours, she eventually reappeared without having bought any.

It was Anne's birthday on 26 October and I still remember the look on her face when a man in a brown uniform arrived at our hotel room carrying boxes and boxes of shoes for Anne to try on. It's one of many special memories of our life together.

We were so grateful to my boss to be considerate enough to think that we would enjoy finishing our holiday in Rome, cocooned in five-star luxury! The first of what proved to be many snatched days on the end of business trips.

The following day we were driving to the airport for our return home and we noticed puffs of black smoke coming from the Vatican to indicate that the new Pope had not been chosen yet. The following day, Angelo Giuseppe Roncalli, Cardinal-Priest of Santa Prisca was elected Pope after 11 ballots. He chose the name Pope John XXIII.

We were house hunting before we were married and when we returned to the United Kingdom after our honeymoon, we continued. Our flat in the King's Road, Chelsea, was very spacious but after quite a bit of searching, we found something which we thought better suited our needs at the time and it was in Battersea. That was in the days before Battersea became as fashionable as it is now, although civilisation was only a short trip across Chelsea Bridge!

Anne took to her new role as a 1950s housewife with great gusto, even to the extent of keeping a very detailed record of her income and expenditure. I have to say that she made a surprisingly excellent keeper of the family expenses. We were by no means well off at that time, just like any other normal young married couple and Anne even recalls crossing the bridge to Kings Road, where she knew a very good greengrocer who would sell her of all things, mushroom stalks because the local Chelsea-ites weren't interested in them – when in fact the stalks have a far richer flavour than the rest of the mushroom!

Inevitably, my boss at Alexander Howden's was a guest at our flat and as he and his wife had given us a smart modern coffee percolator as a wedding present, we felt honour bound to roll this item of equipment out at the end of the meal. Our first try with it, disaster, steam everywhere. Mind you, what it did manage to do was to unravel my boss's wife's very tight perm, while we watched in impotent awe until I dived at the plug!

Anne had a secretarial job with Durie and Miller in Sloane Street - £1000 per year - more that I was getting at the time and parked our little car directly under the office, all day, every day. Meanwhile, I used to get a lift with my friend John Le Bas Freeman in what I remember to be a rather swish Austin Healey 3000 which was a lovely easy drive to work – which even in those days was about 3 rungs up the ladder as far as little sports cars go. Nowadays, of course, they're worth an absolute fortune.

It was while we were living in Battersea that with delight it was confirmed that at last, after nearly a year of hoping, a babe was on the way. Anne fell pregnant with our eldest, Jonathan and so we decided that perhaps we should house hunt again and find something a little more substantial. Plus, it was decided that it may be a very good idea to live somewhere near Anne's parents. We house hunted in Sussex and in Surrey.

The house we eventually found, Greylands was in Wivelsfield. It was a lovely family home, the ideal place to raise a family - £4000. (Nowadays we are looking for a second-hand car for that!)

Jonathan was born in 1960, Caroline in 1962 and Jane in 1964 – so as you can imagine, it was a very busy time and in fact, by the time Caroline was born in 1962, I was made a director of Alexander Howden Ltd. Anne used to tease me about the fact that I felt that I possibly didn't have the necessary gravitas for such a senior job so, I grew a moustache in order to make myself look a little bit older. I was totally thrilled to have been made a director of Alexander Howden Ltd, because those were the days of *my word is my bond*, real propriety and what I call the proper traditional Howden's before all the happenings and shenanigans which ultimately led to its demise – but more of that later.

Ten years later, having built on a large kitchen and fourth bedroom and bathroom and installed central heating and also invested £2000 in half the adjoining field and even built a swimming pool, we were house-hunting again.

I'm very conscious when writing this that in trying to telescope the timeline, I may be giving the impression that we moved house every five minutes, but in fact it was 1968 when we decided that we wanted to go house hunting again. That was the time when our fourth child, Willie arrived. A church friend, Mr Moore asked us at Willie's christening whether we were considering the idea of buying a bigger house

Mr Moore was an estate agent and was extremely helpful. We looked at Malling Deanery, Iford Manor, Lockes Manor and other places because we knew our overseas business friends loved to be welcomed to stay (all under £25,000). We agreed a price on 'Townings', also in Wivelsfield with a pig-farm attached, that was particularly interesting as Anne learnt a lot so that she could support the pig manager which stood her in good stead when finally we made our move to what was to become our final move and what I can only describe as the move of a lifetime - to the property in which we spent the next 20 odd years. However, there was still a process to be gone through.

Our local circle was comparatively small and Willie's godmother, having initially dismissed it, decided that they did want to buy 'Townings'. We lost the negotiation but it was a blessing in disguise.

We went to see Strutt and Parker, a big local country estate agents and I clearly remember talking to a Mr Colvin and telling him we were looking for a larger house and I can quote Anne directly when she gave the following worryingly non-specific instructions to Mr Colvin: *"We are looking for a big house and we don't mind what it costs."* Help!

This time we decided to be as discreet as possible and not tell anyone of our plans or if we had found a property until we had actually completed the sale.

Within a few days we had received particulars of the property which was to become such a very large part of our lives. It was in Firle, East Sussex and it was called "Gibraltar".

The only person we told that we were hoping to buy Gibraltar, having immediately offered the asking price £17500 and been accepted, Anne did tell our special friend Sue Calver, whose sister-in law also pictured living there! We managed to avoid a contract race or bidding war, and eventually I am pleased to report that this was the property which became our home for most of our life together.

We bought the house plus 2 ½ acres of farm buildings and the Gribble family who had been tenant farmers within the property for many years were extremely helpful during the transitional period, which I have to say appeared to go on for years and years. Although the property was quite habitable, it did require quite a few modifications and additions. For instance, since Elizabethan times, the various occupants of Gibraltar had relied on fires for heating and as this was the second half of the 20th century, we decided that we would have central heating installed. Believe it or not, that took nearly 2 years to complete!

In addition to the house, the gardens needed to be gently renovated and we were lucky that our gardener from Greylands , Mr Woolgar, decided he would enjoy the challenge of it all. So the Wednesday trip to collect him from Turner's Hill now took an hour each day but the pleasure of his company and his quiet expertise was very special.

We look back with some concern to the first summer that we entered for the Glynde Flower Show. We scooped lots of special awards, little knowing of the continuing tension between Glynde and Firle and blissfully unaware in our delight of the mutterings that must have been going on!

Gibraltar

I recall someone once saying *there are three of us in this marriage"*. Our own 'menage a trois' consisted of myself, Anne and our beautiful house. It really did become the centre of our lives. Here's a short verse I wrote in its honour;

May hearts enfold.
And in Gibraltar peace
Forever hold
With in our home.
The love that I renew this day
Which is for you and is for aye
Bright in sweet Sussex shine.
A beacon for our children and our time

Gibraltar was a big farmhouse of Elizabethan origin. The house has grown organically over hundreds of years, rather than having had the benefit of an architect's ruler and pencil plus, at some stage in its history, a rather incongruous white Doric portico had been stuck on the front of the building which surprisingly enough, added rather than detracted to its charm and made it unique.

We purchased the property from the Firle Estate and as it had never been sold and had always been a tenanted farm, there were no deeds. In addition to the 2 acre garden and farm buildings, we acquired 5 ½ acres of land surrounding the buildings as well as a further 7 ½ acres at Crossways, 6 acres in Front Field on an agricultural tenancy and 6 ½ acres on an annual grazing tenancy in Burgess Platt. Suddenly, we had a huge farmhouse and 25 acres.

We eventually converted the granary into two self-contained flats. Although there were also all sorts of restrictions and covenants that could have caused many problems as we very soon developed the trust of the Gage family which matured into friendship. To put it in traditional terms, the Lords of the manor and owners of the Firle Estates.

One of the more unusual aspects of the property was the fact that it had the benefit of its own well, so both the house and the farm can be supplied independently of mains water.

My own ambition was to restore the house to as near its original state as possible, but to include all modern amenities available. I've already mentioned the non-existent central heating, and unfortunately we undertook the project of installing the heating just at the time when massive changes were taking place, and imperial and metric threads were being used contemporaneously, so you can imagine both us and the plumbers having to deal with all sorts of problems associated with the two standards.

The central heating was a bit of an ongoing project and because the very extensive pipework involved both excavation and drilling through walls it was something which needed to be completed as soon as possible.

The outside renovations to the garden and the grounds are too numerous to mention, but I will say that we planted about 500 trees around the borders of the front field as well as substantive modifications to the drainage.

I think I can safely say that during our time at Gibraltar, the property underwent a complete restoration inside and out.

It sometimes caused confusion when I would say, *'I'm off to Gibraltar'*, so I think the derivation of the farm's name deserves some explanation. Although there are several versions, here is the most logical and well known:

This version is in the handwriting of one of the earlier vicars of Firle - I believe it was William Crawley (1878 to 1899) who concerned himself mostly with researching Roman remains in the area, but he also referred specifically to the origin of the name Gibraltar Farmhouse, as follows:

'At the time of the siege of Gibraltar (1779-17830), most of the men taking part came from Sussex (see Heathfield tower where many are listed) so that after the siege they remained there and were apparently under the control of the then Lord Gage. He was also reputed to have taken a number of his own staff with him to act as servants whilst out there. He left Sir William Gage, his son, in charge of Firle Place and his son had an affair with one of the housemates. She was then supposedly dispatched to Gibraltar in order to avoid embarrassment. Neither she nor her mother were ever seen again. At least nine months later it was discovered that she was living in the upstairs room at Gibraltar Farm, the room being panelled with panelling, taken from Firle Place and Firle Place fireplace (which would not of course normally have formed part of the furniture of one of the tenanted farms unless of course this was in fact done at the time

of Napoleon's visit). However, the vicar recorded that when the affair became public knowledge. The villagers all said 'She's the one that went to Gibraltar' or 'His Lordship is off to Gibraltar!" From then on, it became known as Gibraltar!

Quite a racy explanation, but it is the one which is generally accepted. The other lesson we learned from that particular anecdote is that when you live in a village as small as Firle......you may fairly expect to be able to keep a secret – but only for a very finite amount of time!

Needless to say, when the Barnes-Yallowley family were living at Gibraltar, there were absolutely no scandals or 'goings-on' and we all remember it as a very noisy, happy and sunny house, always full of people either coming to lunch, supper or even the weekend and generally taking advantage of all the amenities which we had either restored or installed. Our guests would range from our friends in the village right up to the chairman of Lloyds of London.

Many of my work colleagues came to know Gibraltar very well after quite a few visits and I remember our children being terribly excited when certain individuals were about to arrive because we all knew that we were in for an action-packed time. There is one particular individual whose professional life became very closely linked with my own and unknown to us at the time, ultimately our lives would never be the same.

If you'll allow me to fast-forward a few years, one of our greatness sadnesses was the day we had to move out of Gibraltar. It was a tragedy both for Anne and myself, although to this day, it does remain within the family, having been handed down to the next generation.

Here's my description of Gibraltar written at that time. I think that it is an important enough Sussex Farmhouse to be recorded and I hope, if you are not a historian or a builder, that you will excuse some of the more esoteric information contained within the next few pages.

I make no apologies for dwelling on Gibraltar as it witnessed both the best and the worst of our life experiences and I have included some of the thoughts which resulted from the traumas of our final years there:

In 1970 when Anne and I purchased Gibraltar Farm from the Firle Estate.there were no deeds as it had never been sold before and had always been a tenanted farm on the Firle Estate. Besides the freehold of the farmhouse with its 2.acre garden and the farm buildings we acquired freehold an area of 5.5 acres around the buildings with a further 7.5 acres in Crossways and 6 acres in Front Field on a agricultural tenancy and 6.5 acres on an annual grazing tenancy in Burgess Platt, making a total of 25 acres in all.

There were a number of covenants, mainly relating to the fact that the house and buildings should be kept as one unit and used as a family house with farming activities. Restrictions on caravans in the field and similar matters were covenanted but, on the whole, these have caused little trouble and the changeover of one of the buildings, namely the Granary, into 2 self-catering flats presented little difficulty and was handled for us with the Estate by Adams & Remers and Strutt & Parker, in close association with the Gage family. It was also agreed that, although part of Front Field was freehold and part was tenanted it would not be necessary to place a fence across marking the line.

The farm is connected to a septic tank in the farmyard between the Tythe barn and the round barn which has an overflow and a manhole out towards the main road, which was not the case when we arrived, as the main road had not then been built. The majority of the house drainage goes towards the main drains, which run through our part of Front Field, roughly in line with the manhole. We receive water in that from the Firle Estate water supply, our own water coming from a well just outside the dining room window and a short distance from the gate into the swimming pool. This is indicated by a depression in the land and is drawn up by a pump house about 3 - 4 yards from it.

Shortly after we arrived, we dug up the grass and opened the well, which is covered by a large 'stone plate'. Water is drawn up by the two pumps separately with foot valves from a relatively small amount of water in a relatively shallow well, about 9-12 ft. deep. It is apparently constructed on the line between clay and chalk and has a constant flow of fresh water which has never been known to fail in all the days that the Gribbles, both Douglas Gribble and his father were here, through drought or any other weather.

It has also supplied the water for what we now call Farm Office which, by observation, will be seen to have been the Pump House with water storage on the top floor. This was used for the milking herd which gathered in that yard and took water from the trough, which has recently been filled in. We have replaced the farm water storage with water storage in a cistern which is also used as a swimming pool. One pump supplies the house and one the farm, via the dairy, which is pressure pumped back to the converted Granary.

The Pump House also has a hand pump which will pump water into either cistern should the electricity fail. This is regulated by a series of valves and a short extra length of piping to cut out whichever electric pump is not in use.

When considering the changes made to the house by us after we arrived, it is necessary to know that when Douglas Gribble's family lived here, his mother was still alive and she inhabited the south end of the building, more or less as a private apartment.

The area with raised floor in the Cress Room, through the open beam work, was her kitchen with one small kitchen window and a window over the sink which was lowered to open into double doors. Douglas Gribble said there used to be a small cellar under that floor which he filled in and behind the plaster board on the wall, a 'wig post'. We removed plaster from the beams separating the rooms, retaining the beams as they were, with the exception of the main opening which, having been cut out, was replaced in the wall at the end of what was a corridor in the dining room. The dining room had its beamed wall enclosed and a brick paved corridor running through it. The entrance to the dining room was from the hall where there is now shelves for china plates. We restructured this to draw the passageway into the room to enlarge it in a similar way to which we enlarged the Cress Room. The advantage of this was that by extending the conservatory into a full length garden room we linked the two rooms together.

The garden room was to my own design, the idea of the loops of the wooden paling on the outside over the arched doors coming from the paling which existed on the railway station at Lewes and was a Victorian style and appeared to fit the old style of the existing conservatory.

We slated the roof as a number of the farm buildings had slated extensions to tiled roofs. This also meant that the garden room did not get too hot in summer.

It should be noted that the main drain which is in the terrace outside the downstairs lavatory, formerly the butler's pantry with china and wine stored in it, runs along the west side of the wall and then underneath the new garden room to reach the man hole to the east of the down pipe, which is encased in the middle of the garden room.

To open it, it would be necessary to raise some of the floor tiles. The number of these for purposes of record are pencilled on to the top of the lintel for the double doors into the Cress Room. This drain then goes out to the collection point underneath the juniper tree and eventually across the garden to join the main drains.

Small changes were made in the kitchen, enabling a small larder to be cut into what was the downstairs back lavatory. Otherwise the main kitchen is very much as it was, except that in the days of Douglas Gribble this was a sitting room and he remembered his father used to pay the men as they walked past the end window above what is now the kitchen sink.

In those days, the Gribbles' kitchen was in what is now my study and the main dining room was in the Horn Room. The area where the swimming pool is was used for rearing chicks in sheds and also looking after other ill animals. The changing room, which has bars at the window, was the apple store. I was told by the Gribbles that the bars were there because in the days when apples were stored, they were usually stored in a sulphur gas to preserve the apples, hence the windows were barred so as not to be opened mistakenly.

The Pump House was also a little larger and we had to take backwards the front wall; it was formerly covered with corrugated iron and has now been slated with original barn slates. The doorway into the garden through the swimming pool is new.

As can be seen from the windows of the Horn room, particularly towards the garden and to some extent towards the swimming pool, the room is well below the level of the ground. This is believed to have been due to the accumulation of ground over the ages, the house being believed to be of Elizabethan date, ie late 1500s, although Strutt & Parker believe it is late 1600 hence our general reference to it being 17th Century.

Douglas Gribble told me that there was an air raid shelter connected to the Horn Room under the arbour where we now have vines and a small terrace and the entrance to the swimming pool. The Horn Room had the inglenook fireplace completely filled in with a small modern fireplace level with the front of the wall. We noted that the beam over the wall is a concrete team and not a wooden one. Douglas Gribble confirmed that a fire in the Victorian fireplace had burned the beam out and the whole of the front wall was replaced with reinforced concrete by the Estate workmen.

We wished to bring the house back as much as possible to its original state and therefore decided to excavate into the inglenook fireplace. We found another fireplace, probably early Victorian, about 2 feet in and after further excavation we came across the small bricks which are now the back of the current inglenook fireplace. A number of these are relatively small, and when shown to a conservation expert, were expressed to be Elizabethan bricks. They also have a small portion of the original plaster rendering on them to the left.

The wall to the extreme left is new as are the pillars which were put in, in case support was needed for the new beam, as this was an unknown factor and our architect told us there was no way of proving it other than running the risk of the whole thing collapsing from the obviously considerable weight over the new concrete beam, because the existing beam was linked to the main beam in the roof of the Horn Room.

When we excavated we discovered an arched oven on the left hand side, with hooks and hanging spaces and a smoking archway on the right. I don't believe either to these were 'bread' ovens but I think they were ovens for the purposes of smoking meat.

The chimney is extremely big and takes an immediate turn to the right onto a flat ledge about 8ft up and from then on straight up to the roof. It is large enough for a man to climb up inside, in fact we have done this, and it still has the pegs to enable you to climb the chimney. It is joined by the chimney from the kitchen, which has a small slate over the point of which it joins, the four in fact joining much higher up.

We have had a lot of trouble with smoking from the chimney, which requires either a special form of cowl on the top and/or maybe some form of electric fan to keep the smoke rising when the chimney is cold. We were also told that the gap between the hood and the actual fire was too great and should have been a maximum of not more that 2ft 6 ins.

There was no central heating when we arrived and we put full central heating in the house. This involved an enormous amount of pipe work and considerable problems ensued as a number of metric threads were being introduced, although England was still in the main on feet and inches.

The floor in the hall which had to be excavated in small areas to put in the hot water radiator pipes was found to be old hand made tiles, flat on earth, and they were replaced "as is" with a certain amount of sand underneath.

We had a number of holes drilled in two side walls (away from the fireplace and towards the swimming pool) of the Horn Room, because of the wall being below ground. Although there was no obvious rising damp, the holes appear to have checked this. Similar holes can be observed in the garden room, drilled into the wall of the Crest room.

Upstairs we made a number of other changes. The bathroom in our bedroom led straight into the hall through what is now the linen cupboard. In the bottom of the linen cupboard are the steps which led into the bathroom.

We opened up the cupboard under the eaves for the clothes cupboard which was not there previously, as we also opened up the cupboard under the eaves in 'Lily', which was originally Carro's room. Our main problem was the top hall, because here the room which is now called 'Rose',(or the main guest room), stretched right across the building with windows to the front of the house only and a wall across the wooden framework at the west side of the house.

When you came up the stairs, you entered from the top of the stairs through a doorway to prevent draughts, and the whole of the top of the stairwell was enclosed right up to ceiling height, i.e. there were no bannisters.

The bannisters we have put in were copied from those at the bottom of the stairs and the stairs rising to the second floor, and we put in a new wall, which was part bookcase, to provide a library and to provide access to 'Ilex' without have to go through 'Rose'. We then effectively turned both 'Ilex' and 'Rose' round by introducing two dormer windows in the 'catsleap' roof for which we had to get special permission, as Gibraltar is a Grade II listed building just outside a conservation area.

The porch is separately listed. Approval for this work was obtained by our architect and also specifications as regards the exact details for windows and the size of the new panes. At this time we also replaced the windows in the bathroom and in 'Lily' which were previously iron windows of a late 1900s variety and totally out of keeping with the rest of the house.

We cut 'Lily' in half to make the new bathroom for 'Rose' and, as we then had small children, installed two basins in it. Outside we also completely re-tiled the hung tiles with hand made clays from Clayton surrounding our own bedrooms, i.e. in the front or east side of the house. We also repaired the existing tiles hung to the west side over 'Lily' and 'Jasmine'.

When we removed the tiles, which were nearly all broken in front of the house, it was found that there was an oak beam structure of Elizabethan type underneath, but most of the in-filling had been either eaten away by birds or just disintegrated over the years. It was consequently re-lined with a heavy felt, one side silver, replaced under the new tile hanging.

Two final changes were brought about to the house much later on. One was to utilise the roof space between 'Ilex' and the back stairs to form a small bathroom and another was to form a small bathroom in what was the top of the stair space in front of 'Jasmine', which had previously been a cupboard for Jane's clothes.

We also floored in part of the roof near where the tanks are and replaced the hot and cold water tanks. We replaced a large amount of electrical wiring, although not all. There are now two main electrical boards, one off the bathroom from 'Ilex' and one off the second floor near to the stairhead.

In the garden, the front garden is more of less as it was except for the fact that the yews have all been turned into sculptured trees, where they were previously just left to grow. Equally the yews in the rest of the garden have now been cut into shapes.

The main lawn, which was a tennis lawn, is still as it was with a box hedge and herbaceous border, virtually unchanged. The vegetable garden has been wired and enclosed and reduced in size and to the left of the lover's walk (which was here in the Gribbles' days) we have made a new garden outside of the garden room to sit in privately, where there was previously a shed to keep odd tools.

This is beside the outside loo, which is still connected to the main drain, although water has to be brought via a bucket, there being no water laid on. It was said that in the old days, the farmer used to sit on the 'thunder box' still there, with a shotgun across his knees, so that he could shoot the odd passing pigeon, whilst he contemplated nature in the early morning!

A photograph of the privy at Gibraltar Farm mentioning the quality ceramic bowl with a Dombey trademark can be seen on page 30 of the book on Sussex Privies written by David Arscott, published by Countryside Books, Newbury, Berkshire. The rest of the garden on that side, i.e. to the left of the Lover's Walk or the south east of Lover's Walk is effectively new.

The whole of the yew hedge and the whole of the herb garden is entirely our work as is the rose arbour at the end over the gazebo built by Jonathan and the new box hedge under the gazebo. Our final intention is to have the large lawn with its new yew hedge, which is shaped in size of a double square, laid out possibly with a fountain and bushes in the centre and a number of specimen trees down each side, similar to part of the garden at Mount Harry, which belongs to Tim and Alice Renton.

It is the intention to use the rough grass at the end of the vegetable garden and by Lottie's little house, to put in fruit trees which will also reduce the wind from the south west. We have planted several hundred trees, about 500 in all, mostly around the borders of Front Field and in and around Lottie's house and all along the side of the front drive, to the farm drive.

We put new drainage into the old granary before converting the flats, which we did ourselves and which was duly approved and connected to the main drain outside the back door. This area used to be a tip for old wood and farm implements and has now been thoroughly cleared out and the grass restored. There are still, however, some stones under it from the days when it was used as a yard for farm animals; also there is now the power and water for the Granary flats. All the old implements are in the Tithe barn, which we hope will one day form part of a museum of locally used implements.

The drains around the farm buildings are quite interesting and a brief note on them should be made for future record. The main cesspit drain is very close to the Tythe barn and the gate into the Front Field. This has an access plate which is covered by a concrete slab and when this was last cleaned out there was almost a room underneath the yard. It was completely sucked out by the cleaning tanker and the man who did it for us went down and had a look around and announced that it was in a very good state.

A series of drains also cross from the dairy towards the front of the Shire Stable. Just in front of the corner is the entrance to a manhole, which goes down quite a distance, at least six feet. A main drain runs straight through it, across the yard, to a point where the yard gate opens towards Front Field and on the right of this is an even deeper manhole.

These in turn lead to the main Firle drains which run across the field, some ten yards from our drive. These were recently checked (1992) by the Borough Surveyors with a video camera which passed the whole length of the drains and although they are of some age, probably Victorian, they were expressed to be in reasonable condition.

The remaining manhole of interest is between the two garages, one of which is now demolished, which is covered with large bricks. The vent for this is on the wall by the remaining garage and the other vent for the main drain is on a standing column just behind the entrance from Front Field to the main yard.

The drain outside the study window in the swimming pool area runs under the house into the drain beside the swimming pool and pumps under the floor of the boot room and out to the main drain outside the back door, which also connects with the drain from the office and from the Granary flat.

The water for the office is different from the Granary flats. It derives from the pipe near the swimming pool pumping equipment, which passes into the office in the corner nearest the back door and is only triggered when the pump works to supply water to the cistern in the top of the main house. When this happens the cistern in the office fills up. As there is fairly frequent use in the main house, the cistern in the office has worked reasonably well.

A matter of particular interest in the ageing of the house, besides the bricks already mentioned in the inglenook in the Horn Room, is the in-fill between the beams in the entrance from our bathroom to our dressing room cupboard behind our bedroom. That is still full of daub and wattle and appears to be of the origin of the house and, although we have not had it dated, would be a useful way of dating that part of it.

As was mentioned earlier, the general belief is that the house dates from late Elizabethan 1500s, although this has not yet been proved. The beams are of enormous size, particularly those in the Cress Room, which go right up to the top of the house and the beams supporting the 'Rose' bedroom above the Horn Room.

The only room which has any original oak flooring in it is 'Ilex'. Some of the walls are of great width, particularly those in the Horn Room and it is interesting to note that in 'Ilex' under the window facing to the east are some very substantial stones, something like 1'6" x 1' x 1', which are obviously of great age in the construction of the house.

It appears that the house was a typical timber framed farmhouse of the period built by laying the timber frames in four directions and then drawing them together and pegging them and then in-filling the gaps with daub and wattle, stone and other material. And that the outside, i.e. the bricks and/or tile hung and/or flints were probably later additions to protect the timber frames.

The timbers throughout the house, including in the roof and also of course in the Tythe barn, are of really massive construction. Although they have worn away and been eaten over the period of several hundred years, they still have a good deal of strength in them, as witnessed by the fact that the house virtually shook in the 1987 hurricane but only a few tiles were dislodged and the house appeared to withstand the buffeting of that storm much better than modern houses.

The fireback in the lower Granary is of a royal design, showing Charles I, whereas the fireback in the Horn Room is of the traditional Sussex design, favoured by the Sussex Ironmasters.

We have not made much effort to research the history of the house, but such history as has come our way we should record for future interest. As has already been mentioned, we know this was an early farm on the Firle Estate and one of the major farms beside Place Farm.

The name Gibraltar appears on all of the earliest ordinance surveys that we can find and appears to stem from the siege of Gibraltar in 1704. To commemorate the same event the Gibraltar Tower was also erected at Heathfield. We will return to this matter later in these notes.

In July 1994 I met Prue Maddon of Point View, Western Parade, Emsworth, Hampshire. She was the grand-daughter of Mr. Herbert Wadham who raised South Downs sheep at Gibraltar when he lived there between 1879-1917. After 1917 Gibraltar was farmed by Mr. H. H. Froud, who was subsequently replaced by William Gribble in 1929. Douglas

Gribble followed his father in farming the land on behalf of the Firle Estate when he moved to Beddingham in 1970 and has always remained a very good friend and a great help, as have his continuing family, particularly Edward and Jimmy, who farm in the neighbourhood, Gordon having moved to Laughton.

During our time at Gibraltar, we have been greatly helped by the Higgens family. Di Higgens helped us in the early days, both with pigs and horses, and was a great friend and support to Anne. Di's mother, Mrs. Piper, spent an enormous amount of her time assisting with our children: looking after them when we were away, washing and ironing their clothes, and generally giving them amazing support. Few of them would have ever got to school parties or other events without the support of Mrs. Piper and, indeed, as recently as Carro and Algy's wedding, Mrs. Piper was there to see that everything was as it should be.

Her father had been groom to Lord Gage and their family has been associated with Firle for a number of generations. John Higgen's mother, Grace, looked after the Bloomsbury family at Charleston. This is already well documented and is available from other sources. Mrs. Piper was a mine of information on Firle and characters in Firle, having spent all her life there. She also told us that it was tradition in Firle that Gibraltar had at one time been the home of Napoleon and equally that it was rumoured there had been a passageway from Firle Place down to Gibraltar, across the park.

The latter seems unlikely because of the enormous distance involved, but it is worth recording because it was one of the traditions to which she referred. However, as regards Napoleon, it appears that Napoleon III spent quite a lot of time in this part of Sussex. Reference is made to his relationship with a girl from Patcham in Jasper Riddley's book on Napoleon III but he has no record of where Napoleon lived at the time.

However, Kay Challoner, a leading guide at the Dome and also of Firle Place, told us that in her researches when guiding, she had established that Napoleon III, having had to leave France suddenly at a later date than the Patcham affair, had in fact stayed in a farm in Firle. She felt that the only possible candidate was Gibraltar, which, coincidentally, ties in with the tradition related by Mrs. Piper.

The origins of the name Gibraltar are regularly questioned and new light was thrown on this when I was lent a book by Kara then Viscountess Hampden, which had been in the possession of the Vicarage at Firle, the Vicar then being Mervyn Morgan. Since he and Kara Hampden have both left the area, I have been unable to trace the whereabouts of this book, but it was seen by myself and my wife and we both read it.

It was in the handwriting of one of the earlier Vicars of Firle (probably William Crawley 1878-1899) who carried out a lot of general research, both concerning Roman remains in the area, the burial chambers up at Black Cap, and similar matters. He also referred specifically to the origins of the name Gibraltar Farmhouse and his notes in his own handwriting are referred to earlier in this chapter.

Whether this explanation is true or not, no-one can tell but the Vicar obviously got the story from somewhere as it was current at the time that he was in Firle. So it would appear to have some foundation. We have also been told that there is a house in Gibraltar, or close by on the mainland, which is known as Gage's House.

History, Membership and Tradition

Arma pacis fulcra

Honourable Artillery Company Motto

Earlier I mentioned that I took my wife Anne to the HAC Ball without any form of explanation, so I thought that this may be a good time to explain not only about the Honourable Artillery Company but the various other organisations that I have been involved with during my life – and I'm very glad to say that my relationship with most of them remains in place to this day.

The HAC is the Honourable Artillery Company and you may begin to understand what I mean by the word tradition in that not only was I a member, but so was my father and grandfather. Nowadays, the tradition continues with my son William Barnes Yallowley.

The HAC is one of the oldest military organisations in the world although nowadays it is also a registered charity whose mission is to attend to the 'better defence of the realm'.

Remember on page 19, you saw a photograph of a nine-year-old young man wearing a wig and a tabard? The photograph dates from 1937 which was the 400th anniversary of the granting of a Royal Charter to the Honourable Artillery Company by King Henry VIII. The young boy in the photograph is me and believe it or not I remember that day very clearly because it was my job on that very special anniversary to carry the helmet of the general who was leading the march-past in front of King George V. I was in effect leading the Royal salute.

Regiments of the HAC have fought in both world wars and the modern regiment forms part of the Army reserve and is the oldest regiment in the British Army as well as being the second most senior in the Army reserve.

The official regimental march of the Honourable Artillery Company is 'the British Grenadiers' and I remember hearing it played at the 400th anniversary celebrations as if it were yesterday.

When one works in the City, it is often said *'Oh he is very well connected or he knows people'*. Yes that is very true, but all the wonderful people that you become acquainted with are not necessarily workmates or even people who work within the same sector or industry. Organisation such as the HAC draw their membership from young men and women who are working in and around the city of London and I have to say that I have made many friends and acquaintances through my involvement with organisations such as this.

Although the HAC was granted its Royal Charter by Henry VIII, it can trace its history as far back as 1087 and was known under several names but it wasn't referred to as the Honourable Artillery Company until 1685 and didn't officially receive the name until 1860, from Queen Victoria.

You can therefore understand that having been in existence for the best part of 1000 years, history and tradition plays a big part in the life and thinking of the HAC. It has a history of which we are all very justifiably proud.

My ancestor Robert Barnes joined the HAC in December 1796. He was married to Jacob Yallowley's daughter, so you can understand my family's long association with the HAC, because seven years later in 1803,

Joseph Yallowley joined the regiment (he was Jacob Yallowley's cousin).....and so began this seven generation connection to the HAC, including myself as well as my son William.

My father Francis and uncle Arthur were also in the HAC and were injured during the First World War and my namesake Capt Hugh Barnes MC died in 1918 fighting for King and country.

Nowadays, the HAC exists to support the regular army and HAC soldiers have been deployed all over the world, including Iraq and Afghanistan. The constant restructuring and downsizing of the army can only mean that the HAC's role can only increase in importance as it has been part of the territorial Army for over 100 years and its first battle honour was in the South African war (1900 – 1902).

Over many years, the Barnes, the Yallowleys and the Barnes Yallowleys have also played an important and constant role in various City Livery companies.

Joseph Yallowley was Master of the Carpenters Livery Company in 1799 as was his son and I was admitted in June 1950 when Robert Cecil Barnes was Master. I am proud to say that I too became Master and continue my association to this day.

Out of twenty six livery companies, ten of them boast Yallowley and Barnes memberships and family associations, ranging from the Distillers to the Paynter-Stainers where even as far back as 1788, Joseph Barnes was Master. That is where the three shields on the Barnes-Yallowley Coat of Arms originate. You can see therefore how important the City is to the Barnes Yallowley family and vice versa!

What I consider to be one of my greatest achievements as a Liveryman is being instrumental in the establishment of the Building Crafts College which is now into its second decade in Stratford. This year it should achieve enrolments of over 1000 students. The college teaches everything from concrete formwork and construction to GCSEs in English and mathematics. Needless to say, Fine Woodworking and Furniture-making are also very high on the agenda!

Although the Craft College was originally established as early as 1893, it wasn't until 2001 that we re-established the college on Carpenters-owned land.

The Building Crafts College was originally founded ias the Building Trades Training School, and was at that time the only school in London for those joining the construction industry. The College continued on its original site in Central London for over 100 years before relocating to this stunning new building in Stratford which opened in September 2001.

The College specialises in what we now call traditional building crafts, particularly bench joinery, fine woodwork, stonemasonry and architectural stone carving. We are introducing sheet leadwork from September.

Our emphasis is on the use of traditional skills but applied in a modern context to enhance the quality of the built environment. We are also keen to re-establish the ethos of the medieval master craftsman, bringing together the technical skills with the wider understanding of the context within which they are applied.

To this end we established a Master Craftsman's Certificate 2 years ago. The College also received full accreditation as a construction CoVE (Centre of Vocational Excellence) earlier this year and we are keen to play our part in the strategic role which this status implies, especially with the land acquired to support the Olympic bid.

The challenges we face in East London and the Thames Gateway are enormous. The scale of the demand is such that we will need to harness all the capacity of existing providers as well as creating new facilities in specialist areas, if we are to ensure not only that local people get the lion's share of the jobs but also that the construction industry can deliver on the whole range of exciting development projects planned for the Thames Gateway.

Beside immediate College activities we are involved in:
COTAC – Conference on Training and Architectural Conservation
Stratford Construction Skills Centre
Canning Town Pre Vocational Training
Learning & Skills Council
Construction Industry Training Board
The need for timber framed houses in Stratford
Setting up starter workshops
Close liaison with schools, especially Carpenters Road Primary School
Carpenters & Docklands Centre
Lower Lea Construction Skills Partnership

So beside the internal College work, we seek involvement in, and sometimes managing, other projects.

We chair an advisory group involving senior people in:

City & Guilds of London Institute
Construction Industry Training Board

English Heritage

Heritage Building Contractors Group

Society for the Protection of Ancient Buildings

Prince's Foundation for Architecture and the Built Environment

With all these activities, we have developed a dedicated team which has increased from 6 to 23 staff in 10 years.

But we have increased student numbers from around 50/60 10 years ago, to over 230 (with a waiting list) for new students **and**, more importantly, reduced the subsidy from the Carpenters' Charitable Trust from approximately £1,500 per student to £250 – an 8 fold reduction, a real record of success.

Looking to the future, we try to make sure that we cater for all the skills required, ranging from traditional building techniques and conventional building services, to modern steel frame construction and pre-fabricated building systems. We must cover technical and professional services and the whole of the construction supply chain.

In terms of out reach, our plan of action encompasses the full spectrum of recruitment and training from schools to adults, and it encourages greater participation by women and ethnic minorities. We therefore seek to:

- Stimulate interest amongst teachers, parents and pupils; run taster courses and pre-vocational training; and ensure that work placements are available for young people entering the industry.

- We seek to sell the construction industry to the best of the school leavers, as well as those who are less academically gifted. We want construction to be the first choice not the last choice of careers.
- We offer construction skills to those on low paid jobs, for example ancillary workers, supermarket shelf stackers and we must up skill the existing construction workforce. We plan for progression to higher level qualifications, such as the Master Craftsman Certificate, if we are to convince young people that the industry can offer a full career.
- We also engage the disadvantaged and adult unemployed, but we must also help adults who are changing career or returning to work.

The picture painted is one of a wide range of skills which will have to be met by an equally diverse set of target groups within our local communities. It is a complex picture of many interlocking pieces; we have to ensure that the jigsaw fits together.

The Building Crafts College, and hence the Carpenters' Livery, is a leader in craft education and the 14 construction related Liveries. We look forward to working closely with the CLS and the exciting challenges that lie ahead, and trust that the College can play a major role in education within the construction industry.

To this day I take great pride in my involvement in the Building Crafts College and continue to maintain contact with both staff and pupils.

The City of London's primary decision-making body is the court of the Common Council. I was privileged to be elected a member in 1986 and became very involved in all the goings-on in the City after the many changes which were taking place as a result of the 'big bang'.

At the time I was also on the Guildhall School of Music and Drama committee and as I recall at the time of my election to the Common Council, I was deputy chairman.

In all, I was involved with three schools connected with the City of London and my particular interest at the time was working with the Irish society, specifically concerning myself with the performance of schools in Northern Ireland.

Being a member of the Common Council is a great privilege because there are only 100 Common Councilman in the city of London with 25 aldermen representing 25 wards. I was a member of Coleman Street Ward Club and in fact was elected as Chairman. One is elected to the Common Council through the ward and elections take place every four years, although I served on the Common Council for 14 years until my resignation in 2001.

You mustn't for one moment imagine that being involved in the Carpenters Livery company, the Honourable Artillery Company, the Common Council, several schools etc was all committee meetings and cups of tea! There were obviously some perks and one of the most memorable treats that I remember followed a visit that several others from the livery company made to HMS Norfolk in the Pool of London.

It was January 1992 and after we had invited a hundred and twenty of the ship's company to lunch, Capt John Lypiett invited two members of the court for what was known as 'task force orient 92' which involved sailing from Gibraltar to Plymouth.

At the time, NORFOLK was the most up-to-date operational type 23 frigate and we would be sailing alongside the latest carrier Invincible, destroyer Newcastle and several others.

At this time, I was Deputy Master, Vic Brown was Senior Warden and we were both lucky enough to be chosen to make the voyage.

We arrived in a very sunny Gibraltar, were welcomed aboard by the Master at Arms and were ushered onto the bridge where we met the Captain.

If we imagined that this was going to be some sort of 'jolly', we were much mistaken as we spent the next four days on serious manoeuvres as HMS Norfolk was being tested for its effectiveness in its four principal departments. That is to say Operations, Marine engineering, Weapons and Supply as well as the Secretariat. We certainly weren't treated as observing guests but were encouraged to take part in everything that was going on from the fire alarm exercise to learning how to use smoke hoods.

In the evening we dined with the Captain and the senior ratings and that night we had the rather exhilarating experience of being on the bridge as the Norfolk was wound up to full speed and was cruising at nearly 30 knots.

We witnessed the Secretariat (what we might call 'admin' these days) working in very cramped conditions, shuffling paper, reports and inputting information onto their computers (remember this was 1992). It certainly made us think twice about complaining about poor working conditions in the City.

The following day we familiarised ourselves with the weapon systems and even watched a video display of various firings of the ships weapons.

We were even treated to a rather 'hairy' flight in the ship's Lynx helicopter and we weaved in and out of the task force ships with heavy seas running an almost zero visibility – to the extent that there was absolutely no time when we could see all the ships but I'm sure that just for our own entertainment, when we did pass a ship we would carry out a circuit of it at mast height. It was worth going just for that flight – which even rivalled the flight I'd had on American flying Fortress many years earlier.

Inevitably, when travelling from Gibraltar back to the UK, the Bay of Biscay has to be negotiated and this is one expanse of water which does have a little bit of a reputation for unpredictable weather. That particular day was no exception and Invincible had to go to the rescue of a Dutch freighter which had sent out a Mayday. They rescued only seven of the twelve-man crew

The north side of Biscay has much more moderate weather and another one of my abiding memories is our helicopter flying backwards and forwards to and from Culrose as we were almost within sight of England. They were picking up light provisions and post but the greatest surprise was when they bought fresh, hot Cornish pasties onto the bridge as a welcome home.

When almost home, Captain John Lippiett sent out a signal as we steamed through. I found the words very inspirational and have never forgotten it: *'Make way for the seven ships of Task Force Orient so they may salute the Princess Royal!'* I was on the bridge of HMS NORFOLK when he sent that signal.

My great memories of HMS NORFOLK are nearly 25 years old now but I hope they illustrate that any sort of involvement in public service can so often generate those rewards that 'money just can't buy' and makes one's involvement within the fabric of not just the City of London but society in general so rewarding.

Lloyd's of London

"My word is my bond"

You may be wondering why an autobiography contains an entire chapter entitled Lloyd's of London. Well, the fact is that my entire professional career was inextricably linked to Lloyd's and even after I had retired from city life, Lloyd's continued and continues to this day to have a great effect on my life.

The world over, Lloyd's is mostly known for shipping insurance although it is known everywhere as an establishment which will insure just about anything. Lloyd's has always prided itself on the fact that it would accept any risk and when a claim is legitimate, it will always pay out the appropriate sum of money.

Insurance is no more than a rather sophisticated form of gambling and began several hundred years ago when private individuals would even take bets on whether individual soldiers would return from various wars.

Obviously nowadays, it is far more sophisticated and very different.

Massive changes occurred not only to Lloyd's but in the financial markets everywhere during the 1980s. You may recall the Michael Douglas film 'Wall Street', in which the mantra was 'greed is good' and unfortunately several powerful individuals within the City of London adopted that as their own mantra.

As I mentioned before, I was not only chairman or director of several insurance and re-insurance companies but was spending a lot of my time travelling the world and insuring far less sophisticated administrations in the ways of insurance and through so doing, I was introducing them to the Lloyd's market.

The bulk of my career was at Alexander Howden where I rapidly rose through the ranks spreading the insurance and reinsurance word around the world with the byproduct of a lifestyle which would have been envied by most. Everything from holidays abroad, private education to my four children and even to being able to take my family on business trips. I was what is nowadays called a corporate entrepreneur and driving forward the various businesses I was involved with and, I have to say hand on heart, in a proper professional and, most importantly, honest way.

I have to admit that my absences from the city of London meant that I was not completely in tune with all the company politics or the undercurrent of 'non-corporate entrepreneurship' which was seeping into the entire market.

You have to remember that Lloyd's had built its reputation through the tradition of 'my word is my bond' which meant that every transaction carried out was gilt-edged, solid and professionally derived and constructed

I should explain at this stage that insurance is quite a technical subject which relies heavily not only on previous experience of statistical calculations but very often quite exhaustive research on the proposed contract. For instance if someone comes along and wants to insure an aircraft which is about to fly say from London to New York, the odds of it being lost are carefully calculated on previous general experience followed by specific experience related to that aircraft, followed by the value of that aircraft, the number of passengers and their 'value' and a whole host of factors too numerous to list in this book.

The various computations will be carried out by actuaries (who are a cross between an accountant, statistician and a mathematician), the odds would be worked out against a catastrophe and a premium would be derived which was acceptable to both parties.

The risks would be underwritten by what are known as Lloyd's names who have always been liable for the full amount of any claim or at least the proportion which had been negotiated.

Obviously there were occasional losses – that is the very nature of the industry – but historically, Lloyd's names did very well – because they tended to collect more in premium than they ever had to pay out.

The downside for a Lloyd's name is as follows – and remember I'm now going back 30 years or so, so the figures may look a little bit on the small side. I am going back to the time when an average house would cost about £5000.

A Lloyd's name in those days would have to have assets of £75,000. He or she would then deposit about half of that amount which allowed them to underwrite business of approximately £200,000.

The beginning of what would eventually turn into a crisis at Lloyd's began in about 1965 at the time of hurricane Betsy in the United States. Many Lloyd's names suffered quite crippling losses which led to a massive slowing up in new names signing up and established names resigning.

That led to the Cromer report in which it was suggested that the market should be reformed but it wasn't actioned until 20 years later. When the report was finally adopted, a name only had to have assets of

£50,000, would provide a deposit and take on business or risk of up to £350,000. In addition a list of 'mini names' was also created. They only needed assets of £37,500.

By that time property inflation had taken place, many names owned a home which represented quite a sizeable asset and although a home could not be offered directly as an asset, a bank guarantee secured on it could be.

Over the next few years, various mini scandals were apparent at Lloyd's which included 'hiccups' such as certain syndicates refusing to pay out on a claim because they felt that they had been victims of fraud. Underwriters were recommending friends to participate in so-called low-risk baby syndicates and various other activities and schemes were beginning to make the market seem slightly less of the stable entity it had been.

Obviously the old guard were very unhappy about the developments and there were attempts to return the market to its former order and stability and two reports were commissioned which resulted in a chief executive being brought in. He didn't last long but the Lloyd's Act 1982 was enacted which gave Lloyd's certain legal immunities and of course we had the Financial Services Act of 1986.

Those few years of slowly amplifying chaos resulted in a very different type of operator entering the market and the rather staid gentlemanly world of *old* Lloyd's gradually disappeared as (and I hesitate to use the word) bandits moved in and ultimately gained powerful and influential positions in the market.

They had calculated that the market was certainly skewed in favour of the names and Lloyd's itself. That gave the false impression that the risks were lower than they calculated plus they also assumed that if they operated their underwriting like a Ponzi scheme, in that they could write business faster and faster at more and more attractive premiums, the sheer volume of premium income could always be offset against any risks.

Unfortunately, Alexander Howden did not escape as several executives of dubious reputation wormed their way into our very traditional and ultra-conservative business. The majority of the young directors (including myself) fought against the takeover but eventually the ugly spectre of large amounts of cash, promotions and a fresh start proved too tempting. We were dealing with *salesmen* who knew *exactly* how to tell us what we wanted to hear.

The culture of greed and ruthlessness was now firmly embedded not just at Alexander Howden but throughout the whole market and it became very much a case of the survival of the fittest, or more accurately survival of the apparently fittest. Established broking companies were run more like direct sales forces rather than providers of insurance.

Nevertheless, I became a director of the Alexander Howden group and most of us who I have to admit in retrospect, were almost like lambs to the slaughter – innocent as we were of the ruthlessness of modern business practice. We settled into our former routines with a certain amount of initial unease but with the added sparkle of what proved to be fake stardust sprinkled by new boss Kenneth Grob.

Private jets and Dom Perignon soon replaced BOAC and cups of tea.....and I have to admit that far too many of us were seduced.

In essence, my work did not change but the structure of the company did and of course there were those who either left or were culled, especially if the new management felt that they would not fit into the new culture.

I carried on very happily bringing companies together across the world and obviously by doing so increasing my company's revenue which unbeknown to me was being allocated in all manner of creative ways by the new management. The whole operation would culminate in the prosecution of the chairman and one of his underwriters but as often happens, the whole affair took absolutely years and by the time the whole matter appeared to be resolved, time and Lloyd's had moved on and the city as well as the entire financial services industry had become unrecognisable.

Had it been just a case of a rogue underwriter or two, Lloyd's would have survived in its previous form but you have to remember that at the time we were in the middle of the Thatcher years. Reform, modernisation and a new style of management were the flavours of the day.

By that time, I had become a Lloyd's name and effectively had pledged all my and my family's assets against any risks. For a very long time, premiums were rolling in and everything appeared fine. I was not alone.

Tens of thousands of others, tempted by easy money pledged their assets to the insurance market. As a professional, I perhaps should have remembered the old saying *'If something appears too good to be true, it probably is'*..... and so it proved to be the case in the insurance market. Although at the time, it certainly did not *feel* like a bubble which was about to burst.

Nowadays, there are two words which send shivers down my spine: Lloyd's and asbestos.

The fact that asbestos was an accident waiting to happen was nothing new. Many had known for years that everything about asbestos spelt trouble.

The massive health risks were known, although even up to the 1970s, much of the medical profession continued to be in denial but the evidence continued to pile up.

Another red light should have been the fact that it was quite well-known that American insurers would not even contemplate asbestos manufacturers. That is why much of asbestos insurance found its way onto the Lloyd's market.

In 1970 there was what at first appeared to be an insignificant change in American law which allowed private individuals to litigate against asbestos companies. Then followed a 1971 case in the USA brought by an employee against an asbestos manufacturer - which was eventually won by the plaintiff's widow and that, as they say, was the beginning of the end as far as many Lloyd's names were concerned and it led to the destruction of many syndicates. The floodgates had been opened.

Over the previous years, London-based insurance companies had been insuring and reinsuring asbestos-related risks and of course eventually, often following litigation asbestos-related claims began to appear with monotonous regularity and crippling expense.

To a certain extent there was a bit of a rush for the exits and many people in the know managed to dispose of their liabilities but by the same token there are many others who were left holding the baby.

What you have to remember is that in spite of the fact that the Lloyd's market place is a very public place, a brewing catastrophe such as this was very much kept in-house. The outside world was blissfully unaware of the approaching tsunami.

If your name is attached to a certain syndicate, technically you can be liable indefinitely for that syndicate's present and past liabilities unless someone could be found to accept those liabilities.

It is worth mentioning that while all this was happening, new recruits were still being taken on and in 1988, Lloyd's membership peaked at about 32,500. In 1946 membership had been less than 2000.

There were accusations that more and more names had been taken on in order to spread the risk and dilute liabilities.

However to be quite frank, names such as myself were stuck. All we could do was watch the horror unfold and our assets gradually dissipate. Although membership of Lloyd's peaked in 1988, year and total losses were approximately £500,000,000. By 1993 the losses were £3,000,000,000.

Life was unravelling for thousands of Lloyd's names. Many of us were trapped on what is known as an 'open year' and many of us were members of several syndicates.

70% of the losses suffered by 30% of the names, resulting in about 500 bankruptcies, many suicides (some of who were friends of mine) with many names realising that they would probably have to lead the rest of their lives in much reduced circumstances. Many lost their homes.

Prosecutions, talk of conspiracy and recrimination did nothing to help those of us who had been so badly burned.
The *real* reason for everything that happened was no more than appalling management and extremely weak control systems.

The Lloyd's collapse brought about a seachange in faith for me and many others who now accept that there are other things beside material success. It is very easy to philosophise after the event but when you're actually a passenger on a runaway express train it is extremely difficult to climb off until it stops.

The question I often ask myself nowadays is whether we are indeed entitled to guaranteed profits for what is in reality very little effort? My instincts tell me 'No!'

One great byproduct of the whole terrible experience was the simplest of all things. It was the kindness of our friends and people who knew and appeared to understand what we'd been going through.

Luckily, although our self-esteem took a terrible battering, thankfully, our esteem in the eyes of others remains intact and clearly shows the compassion and humanity of the community in which we are lucky to find ourselves.

And for that we continue to be very grateful....and in that spirit, the following chapter is entitled *"A Lententide Contemplation"* which I wrote after our experience – an experience which not only reaffirmed our faith but at a comparatively late stage in life gave us the opportunity to reassess almost everything .

A Lententide Contemplation

"Prayer is not asking. It is a longing of the soul. It is daily admission of one's weakness. It is better in prayer to have a heart without words than words without a heart."

Mahatma Gandhi

To contemplate faith is to think together about the journey which we all experience within our lives. In many ways, it's the little words that count. The small adverbs and when we consider faith, we can think of it in so many different ways. By faith, or with faith, or of faith or in faith so many writers tell us about how they seek a land which is not really known to them but which they contemplate through faith.

From these writers we get quick flashes of insight into their views: C S Lewis' "Out of the Silent Planet", or "The Lion, the Witch and the Wardrobe", Charles Morgan's "The Voyage" and Dickens' "Tale of Two Cities". Where Sidney Carlton starts his tale from "It was the best of times and the worst of times." and finishes with the last lines of the book "It is a far better place that I go to than I have ever known." "Alice's Adventures through the Looking Glass" also takes us to an unknown world as does Bilbo Baggins in "The Lord of the Rings", and Francis Thompson in his amazing poem "Where He is pursued by the Hound of Heaven". Most of the books are strangely enough children's books and possibly this is because when we are children we can have the faith which we can hardly dare to contemplate in our later life.

So, where does my story start? Well, like all stories we need to consider its background and so we have to retrace our steps back to the reign of Queen Victoria in 1894 when my father arrived on this planet.

Shortly afterwards he wrote an essay on Bleriot's just completed flight over the channel.

In 1914 he was in France unbelievably with his own horse, Queenie, and still carrying a sword. He told me later that it was by faith that he survived those appalling days at Mons and the Somme where he was successively shot in the leg and later blown up by a shell. Each time he returned to the Front with his two brothers: Arthur and Hugh, his younger brother, who was shortly to be killed by a mortar shell after being awarded the Military Cross.

Because of this tragedy, my grandfather forbade his remaining two sons to marry on active service. And so my parents eloped and married in a registry office in Rye shortly before he returned to France in 1918. My grandfather was rather serious being an Actuary in the City of London and believed that the City was the place for his sons.

But when my father returned after the War, married, he wanted to put the horrors of the War behind him and went to Sealhayne and took up farming in Cullompton, Devon. Within a few years there was a substantial slump in farming and many farmers, especially those who had only just recently started with small amounts of land, went to the wall. This included my father.

He then had to eat humble pie and ask his father to see if he could get a job, which was extremely difficult in those days. My grandfather as the Actuary of the Phoenix Insurance Company found my father a job in insurance at which he succeeded but it was never to his liking.

My father's eldest brother had 3 girls and his sister also 3 girls, so when I arrived in 1928 (10 years after his marriage in 1918), my grandfather was delighted that he had a grandson and it enabled my father to restore his relationship with his own father. My grandfather was an extremely interesting and intelligent man although a real Victorian and on a number of occasions when I stayed at his house with him on my own, he would discuss all sorts of interesting things.

With cups and saucers and a candle he explained the movements of the planets and the phases of the moon. We made model aeroplanes (a relatively new invention in those days) and he started a Stamp Album for me. He told me a lot of his beliefs in the Divine Creator so that distinctly influenced me in my early life.

As he lived in a Victorian household, we also had daily prayers with all the servants which I subsequently discovered was part of Mattins. This also influenced me as did the fact that my parents attended a Congregational church in Purley which, in the 1930s, was extremely well attended and popular with some 300 people attending the morning services and 150 in the evening. Before the sermon commenced in the church, we, the children (I being between 5 and 8 years old at that time), left to attend the children's church of which there were about 80 of us.

I remember particularly we supported the London Missionary Society and learned a great deal about David Livingstone's work in Africa and at that age church was fun for us and we did not know the difference between the Congregational Church (we never called it Chapel) and the Church of England.

My grandfather told us of an earlier relation of mine, Jacob Yallowley, who lived in Clapham and was part of the Clapham set, which was led by Wilberforce fighting against the slave trade. We all knew that the most important church in England was the City Temple in the City of London and the enormous crowds who attended its services. It was therefore very strange at that age to listen to prayers from the Church of England which my grandfather used, talking about miserable sinners and the resurrection of the body.

Even at 8 years old I was deeply concerned as to why this should be said and who these miserable sinners were and what were their sins, and it seemed ridiculous to think about the resurrection of the body – it didn't fit in with my happy and fulfilling life in the Congregational Church.

As Church was an important factor in our life – by then I had a sister – we often talked on Sundays, when we had a special Sunday meal at lunchtime but always called "dinner", which in those days was chicken or beef, both normally used once a week as a special occasion. This conversation very often took the form of discussions about the earlier church service – what happens to people after they die? And then, for example, what happened to people who died before Christ was born and the problem of the phrase "the resurrection of the body"?

Looking back, I think it is quite interesting how many religious type problems I had as early as 8 years old and I think sometimes today people do not take on the real concerns of the young, especially since sometimes the adults themselves do not have an answer.

I went to a Church of England school where the Headmaster always took all classes for a subject he called Divinity. It was an opportunity for him to discuss all matter of things from our behaviour in school to faith in God and any other matters he felt were relevant. It was in fact a very useful sort of lesson because it did not have any strict format to it and I was interested to learn recently that the Head of Dulwich College at that time also used Divinity as a main subject with similar application. Today things are somewhat restricted by the fixed agenda for lessons from which teachers find it difficult to diverge.

This is however slightly rushing ahead. Before that we had endured the Second World War and almost immediately after its declaration in September 1939, I was in the garden when Croydon Airport was attacked and bombs shattered a number of houses in our street. This was a pretty rude awakening on the life we had lived without that fear.

We moved around to different areas to escape the bombing. First down to Milton-on-Sea near Portsmouth, which of course then became a target, and then back to my aunt's house in Northampton when we were in time to spend most nights in their cellars as the Luftwaffe bombed Coventry, which was directly on the route from Northampton. By that time things in London were a little quieter and my father had built a very substantial air raid shelter under the lawn which he was convinced could only be damaged by a direct hit.

When we came back to Purley we were then in time for the main Blitz on London – not very good for small children. I suppose it does affect your faith dramatically when you are faced with immediate attack, which is not quite the same as the occasional IRA bombings, which one always felt was unlikely to happen to you. In our case when we spent most nights in the shelter, there was a lot of damage in Purley and we could hear the bombs whistling down. I think we all prayed that it would not happen to us but of course one had to face the fact that why should this be so for you and not for others. My mother always cheered us up by saying that God would look after us quoting Psalm 91:

> You will not fear the terror of the night
> nor the arrow that flies by day,
> nor the pestilence that stalks in darkness,
> nor the destruction that wastes at noonday.
>
> A thousand may fall at your side,
> ten thousand at your right hand;
> but it will not come near you.

Later on at school in term time, which was then in Huntingdonshire, we were away from the holiday problems of bombs but we spent quite a lot of time talking about the war and following through the progress of the allies on maps, particularly in the North African campaign.

Besides being in the ATC as I was, some of the senior boys, particularly if they were day boys and lived locally, were in the Home Guard and we had a very dramatic incident when one of the prisoners of war working on a farm went berserk with a knife, was holed up in a local farmhouse and eventually shot by one of our boys who was in the Home Guard. It certainly brought war home to all of us.

We also had, in the later half of the war, a dramatic incident when jet engines had just been invented and the Meteor fighter was in action. One of these planes burst into flames just over the school and crashed at the end of the playing field. And my reactions then are in a poem I wrote at the time ....

In the 1940s there were very few small radios and because the batteries we see today were not developed, all radios apart from those on mains were kept charged with accumulators, which had to be taken to shops to be charged up regularly. Because of the danger of spillage of accumulators most of us made crystal sets, which surprisingly enough could give us quite good reception provided we slung an aerial over the school dormitory and buried a substantial earth in the ground, usually a wire soldered on to a biscuit tin. This enabled us with ear phones – strictly forbidden – to spend a long time in the evening before we fell asleep listening to the American Forces network.

At school, again in Huntingdonshire ,I was away from the holiday problems of bombs and we spent a lot of time talking about Einstein's Theory of Relativity and battled with the problems of the speed of light. I particularly remember reading a book called "Dunne's Experiment with Time" which although not religious seem to have strong applications with time and space. I recall short poems which encapsulated some of these thoughts:

"There was a young man who saw God,
Must think it exceedingly odd,
If he finds that this tree
Continues to be
When there's no-one about in the Quad."

and of course the reply was:

"Dear Sir

Your astonishment's odd

I am always about in the Quad

And that's why this tree

Will continue to be

Since observed

By yours faithfully

God."

And similarly on relativity:

"There once was a lady named Bright

Who could travel much faster than Light.

She started one day

In the relative way

And arrived the previous night!"

And so besides these discussions, sometimes deep and sometimes very irreverent, we also had a lot of adventure and fun as well. They recently made a film on the American Flying Fortress called 'Memphis Belle' that reminded me that as members of the Air Training Corps we used to fly with the USAAF and although because of the war we were not allowed to fly with them outside this country, we were nevertheless all trained as waist gunners in case we were attacked (as one was) in the North Sea when they went out on practice bombing runs.

It makes you 'grow up' quickly at 16.

I recall that on my first flight with the Flying Fortress the pilot, who had just returned from leave in the US, said in a deep southern twang through my earphone as we raced down the runway "Oh God I hope I can remember how to get this crate off the ground". A throwaway line but one which made you say a quick prayer! And then suddenly there was a space above you as you looked down through the open bomb doors.

Later on I did National Service in the Airforce, mainly radar work on isolated hills in the south of England, and then monitoring Russian aircraft during the Berlin airlift.

After that Cambridge and the difficult decision for almost all teenagers, what on earth do I want to read? The decision was made for you if you wanted to become a cleric or a lawyer but the rest was wide open although in those days you could only read a classical form of study and if you were going into business there was really no choice except political economy as the nearest thing to suit one for a business career.

It turned out to be very helpful for my life in the City but with hindsight the most important thing one discovered was how to learn rather than what to learn and in later life I would probably have chosen archeaology. My tutor was the grandson of the great Cambridge economist Alfred Marshall and so his views on life and living had quite an effect on me, as did Maynard Keynes who was then influencing the relationship between America and England in a big way which of course led me to learn something about the Bloomsbury set, who lived close to Firle at Charleston and of which Keynes was a leading figure.

Recently we have had the trial of Blunt as 'the third man' and he was one of the leaders of a society called The Apostles, a member of which was one of my tutors so you can imagine that his interests, both philosophically and on life in general, were very diverse.

When I went to Cambridge my headmaster wrote to me and said "Let your eye be single and your whole body filled with light". This is of course a wonderful philosophy but I only think that now as I look back on a fascinating and varied life but hardly with a single purpose.

Besides rowing for one of the Lady Margaret Eights, in those days we were Head of the River and had six in the Blue Boat.

I took a leading part in the Cambridge Christian Union and also in debates at the Union itself. I acted in The Johnian Footlights which was a lesser branch of the main Footlights, where we had such colleagues as Leslie Bricusse, who wrote Salad Days amongst other musical comedies as well as having been involved in the early days of Beyond the Fringe..

I recently met Norman St.-John Stevas who is now Lord Fawsley and we were able to recall our days at Cambridge Union, especially when an outspoken Irishman Devallier spoke on the wickedness of the English in the Irish Question, which was a complete revelation to me at that time.

Emmanuel Church, Cambridge, also played a large part as did the fact that all colleges closed their gates at 10.00 pm and no women were allowed in men's colleges after that time unless by special dispensation, such as a "May Ball". The only way in after 10.00 pm was climbing very difficult fences and in these one had to avoid the Proctors (a senior Dean plus 2 bulldogs, speedy and aggressive college porters). Needless to say, I was captured on one occasion and had to report to the Dean. One felt very much as though one had been summoned to the Headmaster at school so it was quite a surprise when he opened the door with "How nice to see you Mr Barnes. I trust you will enjoy a sherry."

Having disarmed me in this way, he then spoke to me about College rules with interesting asides such as the importance, as he saw it, of the opportunity to "sin" and be caught but to rise again! If nothing is debarred, he asked, where then is the virtue in having any morals? He reminded me of the French quotation "Qui s'excuse tout, s'excuse le Diable lui meme". He stressed therefore that there must be limits which we can exceed, as indeed I did by climbing in.

Do I believe in the Devil? A tricky question. Certainly I believe in temptations which can destroy love and harden the heart. We are surrounded by these choices every day so perhaps *the Devil* is a good composite word for those forces in life which we struggle against and which is epitomised in so many books, such as "The Lord of the Rings", "The Lion, The Witch and The Wardrobe" and Pullen's Trilogy "The Dark Materials".

I think that the Bible is probably right when it states that we struggle against principalities, against powers and the rulers of darkness and spiritual wickedness in high places. Do we have prophets now as they did in the Old Testament? Well of course we have many films and novels about the fight of good and evil so yes, we are still warned to be on our guard.

I left Cambridge determined to do something useful in the world outside and therefore was very happy to find that after a rather boring experience with accountancy, I could join a Lloyds broker, which was then beginning to spread its wings internationally. This gave me an opportunity to travel extensively, largely in relation to large World Bank projects, such as dams and hydro-electric projects, and to build bridges between far off insurers and the London market. It meant a lot of time away from my family, who were then very young, approximately 3 months per year, but it included work in the Argentine and Brazil, Japan and Thailand, Australasia and Canada as well as a major input into Europe, especially Scandinavia.

The motto of Lloyds was "Fidentia" similar to that of the Stock Exchange and the moral standing of Lloyds and the Stock Exchange in those days was high and so it seemed a very appropriately Christian approach to life to travel to involve us in the economies of other countries. Indeed some of the hydro-electric projects did make an enormous difference to life in some counties, such as El Chocon providing hydro-electric power for Buenos Aires, the Mangla Dam in India and the Kariba dam in Africa.

And later on insuring the first of the jumbo jets, problems with oil rigs and later still when I flew to Poland, which was still in the grip of the Iron Curtain, to discuss international re-insurance with them, and to find that when I was taken to the opera by my hosts, almost the whole of the Polish audience were Russian soldiers.

My job was then to arrange international credit insurance in dollars and sterling to enable the Polish economy to buy equipment which could not be bought with their own currency, the zloty. After one of these trips, flying back from Finland, I found myself on a Russian aircraft, no-one speaking English, a far cry from the comfort of international aircraft. Yes, if you wanted a drink, a small glass of water was brought to you together with a copy of their latest 5 year plan. I watched with some concern to make sure the aircraft flew West and not East and as my wife pointed out later, I would have had a lot of explaining to do had I landed in Moscow!

Heady stuff! Three months travelling overseas, but lots of money for schooling, holidays abroad with our four children who I took whenever I could at whatever age, and some delightful au pairs from all parts of the world.

Then catastrophe. Our old distinguished and traditional company was suddenly taken over by a gang of "wise guys" who had a dubious reputation throughout Lloyds. The majority of the young directors fought against the take-over but money will out and the moral traditions of the old company were completely undermined by those who spent their lives in nightclubs, private jets and drinking Dom Perignon at every opportunity on a world wide basis.

In the early days of the 747 one could travel first class in the front of the aircraft and on the upper deck in a Jumbo lounge that was hardly used. It was an amazing experience compared to the push and crowd of current transport. One could walk about after sitting at a coffee table and look out at the polar ice cap as we sped over the globe to Japan or through the Norwegian snow scape.

I spent time in the foothills of the Andes at Bariloche, I met Russians, Poles and Japanese at a time when the war had only shortly ended and few people had any contact with our former enemies. This talk I was asked to give was for the Lenten period and so I can mention that on these longer flights one did have time for deep thought and prayer, beside which there was little in the way of entertainment on those long flights.

I can remember consoling words from a Buddhist monk in Japan at his temple, high Roman Catholicism in Italy, embassy churches spanning the world and on one Sunday, leaving Japan I arrived courtesy of the date line on the same Sunday in San Francisco and heard the great organ in that hill top church pealing out the hymn, as on each continent and island, the dawn leads on another day. The voice of prayer is never silent – deeply moving.

Shortly after I felt the exciting and rewarding work bringing companies together across the world, I was to experience the sadness of greed and complacency in the Lloyds' market. A tragedy for many businesses and for a great number of individuals of about 30 who were reputed to have committed suicide, 3 of them were good friends of mine.

And so a lifetime of work in a sense went up in smoke. It was not just the loss of savings and houses for most people, but also a job which they and I had spent our lives on and which had crumbled. Instead of being able to be proud of one's career, the dreaded word "Lloyds" still sends a shiver down my spine certainly more than my childhood horrors during the Second World War.

My faith was severely tried but fortunately our friends were very good to us and we received very kind counsel from many and wonderful words from my wife when I announced we had lost all our savings. "Darling" she said, "we have our family and our health so let's remember it's only money we have lost."
So I retired early and we worked very hard on the farm at Gibraltar with some 39 sows, producing over 1000 piglets a year, a number of bullocks, frequently as many 30, and up to 80 sheep and 2000 chickens. This kept us very busy but sadly the new regulations in the Common Market ruined the pig market and forced small producers to go to the wall.

So we had a second set of major disappointments and I felt the need to concentrate on some form of charitable work. I had already nearly 30 years experience of running youth clubs called Dockland Settlements in the East End of London where its work was extremely important for the many deprived people and their children, especially as the increasing number of immigrants were now more than the original white population.

I was elected as the Common Councilman for Coleman Street in the City of London and this gave me an opportunity to be elected as governor on several schools where the City had close connections and so influence the Christian nature of education. There were frequently great arguments with other governors who were strong on multi-faith and light on Christian principles, although most of the schools had been founded for that purpose especially for example King Edward's, Whitley, which was established by Edward VI by whose gracious gift the Bridewell Royal Hospital was established.

This was due to the piety and eloquence of Bishop Nicholas Ridley whose sermon moved the King's heart to grant his Royal Palace "as a place to lodge Christ in". There was also the City of London School for Boys and Christ's Hospital, Horsham.

One of my particular pleasures was being elected Chairman of the Building Crafts College in Stratford, a post I held for 10 years during which time the College developed substantially both in instructors and students from 60 students to 230, and its reputation developed both for fine woodwork and stone masonry and later conservation as well as lead work. The College has now become a major charity for the Carpenters Livery Company and has achieved a cove status – a centre for vocational excellence.

The Lloyds collapse brought about a seachange in faith for me and many others who now accept that there are other things besides financial success. We have of course been followed by many other matters of grief: the collapse of Barings, formerly a most prestigious bank, and the worldwide collapse of Enron.

Now we have Rover and the Channel Tunnel so maybe the question is not whether we should concentrate on being financially strong, but morally strong. It seems that many of the problems we have today can be put down to too much materialism and the "I want" complex.

Part of the Lloyds problem also involved the many claims on all sorts of products which when first developed were considered useful and good and then with more knowledge turned out to be things where the insurers were paying for changing in knowledge.

The American Dream has also brought us an increasing litigious society. Are we right to demand compensation for everything which ultimately has to be paid for either by insurance or taxation? Are we entitled to guaranteed profits for life which now appear illusionary for many pension schemes and is this loss of security an acknowledgement of our human frailty and mortality.

I think at that point one of the most telling matters was the welcome of Berwick church which helped to restore faith after we had lost the very wonderful priest at Firle and the new and difficult vicar drove many of us to other churches. So it is also strange that making some notes for this talk I am in the room where Boyes Ellman was born especially as it was he who restored Berwick Church, largely by his own physical efforts.

Our worship at Berwick led to involvement in the Deanery Synod and then later membership of the Diocesan Synod and taking the two year Bishop's course. It then became necessary to take on the role of Church Warden at Firle where it seemed the most important issue was to keep the spirit of the church alive even if not many people came to it, and to concentrate on the restoration fabric so that it's over-1000 year old history would be there for future generations who would surely need it. Perhaps this was also a Boyes Ellman influence.

In conclusion, I would like to share with you two small poems, one of which I was encouraged to write by Jimmy Woodward, the then vicar of Firle and which he used during our Armada service for its 400th anniversary in 1988. May I also share with you an earlier poem which is used at Firle Carol Services and was dedicated to the then Sixth Viscount Gage.

Armada Anniversary Sunday

In this Sanctuary has trembled a spark breaking out as a star in
Eternity and in the timelessness the voice of Firlemen say with the Psalmist
voice of three thousand years ago, "The lot has fallen unto me in a fair
ground, Yea I have a godly heritage."

Climb we the Ancient Downland ways
Where our Stone Age fathers trod.
Seek in the rolling Sussex Downs
The hidden greenways of God.
Lift our eyes to the strong smooth hills
Encircling our homes and lives;
Here is peace and strength to our wills,
And a love that never dies.

Sunrise, sunset, red gold the sky
Rays over sacred Barrows
A beacon of light from on high.
The plough turning life's furrows
As it strikes on the flints of time;
We glimpse in Armada fires
A burning bush and Holy Sign
A spark of the Light Divine.

Safe in the arms decreed by time
Black Cap Down to Caburn Mount
This village lies, a timeless sign
Of our loving God the found
Of living waters flowing true;
Life to sheep and golden grain,
Springs from the wells of downland dew
Our souls washed with Holy Rain.

Now thank the Lord God who made us
To dwell in this pleasant land.
Raise thankful hearts for the blessings
Received from His generous hand.
Climb we the ancient Downland way
Where our stone age fathers trod
Seek in the rolling Sussex Downs
The hidden greenways of God.

Read by Canon J Woodward
Firle Church
1988

A Firle Carol written for the Sixth Viscount Gage

Christmas is dawning,
Like the first morning,
Children are singing
Like the first day.
Let me too praise him,
He who is coming,
Each new renewing
Upon our way.

God is descended
Into each person,
Born in all people
As he first came.
Open your ears then
Like Mother Mary
To angels singing
Glory God's name.

Open your eyes then
As did the sages
To God's great riches
Given for men.
Then let your lips sing
As did the shepherds
Telling of God's peace
Sent now and then.

Thus may we echo
God's new beginning
Offered to all men
Each glad new day
Death, life and rebirth,
His re-creation,
Sing down the ages
Truth is for aye.

Victoria Hospital
1985

Saving the Best until Last – The Family

My family have been the joy and inspiration and at times the challenge of my life. I am so proud of my children and all that they have achieved, enjoyed and enriched my life. I could happily write another couple of books on the wonderful time with them, but that will have to keep for now.

Appendix 1: Wartime Poems

"London's lonely, as the country's homely"

As a leaf, I wander lone
Blown by an autumn breeze,
Blown along the cold grey stone
Of a city street, I freeze.
I freeze for the lack of a friend
The lack of a firm handshake
I feel as though my way I wend
Adrift on an unknown lake.
I am alone, yet in mass,
Of leaves of varied tints,
Alone like some poor country lass
In th'house of a might prince.
Thus, I wandered in a crowd
Of hurrying, scurrying men;
Talking, jostling, noisy and loud
And looking now and then
At a man here or a girl there
With merely a passing glance
Each concern'd with his own affair
And his business life of Chance.
"Can "cars" make friends with me
Or the statue in the square,
Or the Thames, which rolls to th' sea,
Or Wandsworth's commons' fair?
Of City! – how I hate you,
You only stand and stare ...
Have mercy when you view
This poor lone mortal's share."

Now, as a leaf I wander lone,
Or do I tell a lie?
The varied tints now seem to tone
And wind speaks with a sigh;

Here all the world is friendly
In this quaint old village place,
And folks they smile cheerfully
On a strange or unknown face.
They pass the time of day
These yeomen of this land
They guide you on your way
With Christian shake of hand.
Then out upon the highways,
Where few folks seem to pass
'Good morrow friend' the robin says
As he hops across the grass.
The country's friendly in a way
No artist can explain
The sweet perfume of new mown hay
The warm refreshing rain;
The measureless sky of azure hue
Sailed by countless clouds
Billowing sails an ocean of blue
With flapping wispy shrouds.
The stooks of kindly corn
Nodding their heads as they stand,
Glowing red gold at the dawn
Precious fruits of the land.
The chattering friendly brook
Talking all night and day,
Filling each cranny and hook
And gurgling on its way ...
Thus nature proves to me
Its friendliness to man;
Since God has made it free
To aid his mighty plan.   *April 1945*

Victory in Europe Day

The day has come at least
For which we've waited long –
The dice has now been cast,
And Right has conquer'd Wrong.

We're happy now and wine flows free
As it did some years ago
They thought they end of wars they'd see
But blood still had to flow.

They mourn'd as we and danced as we
Lest we shall ere forget
Our children's children we must free
And those they shall beget.

They must not see the sights we know
Women and children killed –
Yet they should stand with heads bow'd low
Knowing how graves were filled.

Forgetting not what we have learnt
From blood and worry and sweat;
The ghastly grotesque forms of the burnt,
The corn fields stained and wet.

The ominous drone of approaching 'planes,
The death from the azure skies,
The men in prison camps in chains,
The worrying waiting wives.

As I write these words, I feel
They're cold and clearly set,
Thus when in prayer we kneel
God grant we'll ne'er forget.   May 1945

"To a Friend"

The finest things are worth so much
And yet they all are free;
But most of them we cannot touch
And few there are we see;
We feel the cool and gentle rain
We hear the birds of song,
We see the azure rolling main
The cedars tall and strong.
But, of the best, of all that's free
Is that which we shall never see,
The faithful bond of friend with friend
Which shall endure until the end
Because it's not of mortal kind
But betwixt the last mind.   *June 1945*

Comes the Dawn

Softly, silently, slowly revealing
Slips the night to the West receding
As on that far Eastern height
The sun stands up in a blaze of light.

The sins of the world with the night are gone
The sun comes up to lead us on;
The fields are clothed in emerald green,
And diamonds glisten where the dew has been.

The spiders web in the morning light
Is as faery lace spun in the night,
And mushrooms stand to tell the tale
Of faery feastings in the dale.

How I love to hear in the cool, fresh morn,
That song of the birds, greeting the dawn,
Those chattering sparrow in the eaves
That singing thrust amongst the leaves.

The sunlight steams thro' the pines on the hill
The copse is silent, fresh and still:
Then, in the scrub, a rabbit stirs
And birds fly out from the neighb'ring firs.

The whinnying horse from across the way –
The sonorous bell greeting the day ...
Giving a message to all God's sons
From the swineherd's boy to the pious nuns.

Let all men marvel at the Dawn of Light,
When fresh hopes shine from out the night
For though that Night may swallow some ...
The rest will stay till the race be run.   *July 1945*

Sarcasm?

You are cruel in your kindness to me
You are too fair in your justity
Your pleasantness is as a pleasantry;
Your faint praise too loud sounds,
It makes my deeds ring hollow:
A more glorious road, leaving thine to wallow
In the dust I've shaken to the ground.   _October 1945_

The Meteor

Men toiled
Horses stirred
The bridle rattled its tune,

Th' ploughshare cut
The soil turned
The sun was at its noon ...

Autumn waited
The leaves fell
The shafts of the sun grew dim

A 'plane roared
The earth shuddered
The smoke was as black as sin ...

A funeral pyre
Of white hot heat
Labourers rushed to the spot

Fire bells clanged
Sirens shrieked
But the flames they noticed not.

Sunset came
A sky of blood
The guard with bayonets stood

For 'neath the turf
A mortal lay,
At least, his mortal hood ...

The dawn rose
On misty heights
The wreck lay, bare, forlorn.

Men lived;
But o'er the sea
Some women now will mourn.

Kimbolton
November 1945

And why 'to War'?

Rearing rocks above splashing surf,
Heather'd heights o'er trespassing turf,
Mighty mountains stately standing.
Seagulls crying, circling, landing;
Tarns on hills, marsh in the glen
This is a land for men.
Here men toil and till the land
Here they work, and understand
The earth is a temple, the skies for a tent
The grass is its carpet, the flowers its scent;
The glorious purple enhanced with gold
The dewdrop diamonds which the sunlight hold,
Are gone in this place where man may dwell
Where he may draw form a living well
Of the highest thoughts that men require,
Those that are of Godly desire.
Loving one's land, and one's brothers too
Giving the world the best one can do.
This is the shape of the Craftsman' plan
Where man must work for the good of man.
By words alone man cannot live,
But from the fruit the field will give;
For by strong arms and heartfelt prayer,
The stones are bread and daily fare.
Thus when the golden grain turns black
And standing fields are beaten flat,
Though Moira may have set the sail,
Or Atropos with shears and scale
Done such as is beyond our ken ...
We know not how, or why, or when?
Then, as a potter turns the clay

Events, as clay are turned His way;
Our empty barns turn their design
To other lands with another clime,
They hope for rich ripe corn do fill
Their empty sacks and disused mill.
Brotherly love on an ocean of strife,
Sharing the chart past the rocks of this life;
Whilst man fights wars he will fight again
For the blood to gush from another vein,
Whist the hydra grows another head
So women again will mourn their dead.
The bow is drawn across the strings
As though to draw the soul, on wings
From out Mars' trophies. Death transfixed
Friend and foe together mixed,
Is blood and mud the dead and living lie,
The stillness broken by the wounded's cry.
That cry which rends the temple veil
And rings o'er hill and quiet dale'
Which to the sleepy world inquiries;
"How can our God allow such fires
As these that are of evil fame,
Our men to kill, and blind and lame."
Still while the scarlet poppy grows'
Men struggle on with mortal blows.
But faithful we, should if we look,
See written in our Holy Book
That God still as a Father cares,
And give us of His Goodness shares ...
For ever whilst blood still flows,
The poppy over Flanders grows.

February 1948

Armistice memorial in today's world

Saturday night and the same again
I loved her then as I love her now
Bird I said what the hells your name
You're a Saturday moll lets do it again
Its always the same on that flaming pad
Its no good crying to Mum and Dad
Who the hell cares now as we roll again
Love I said its always the same.

As a kid I heard of the knight and the maid
Striving for love and finding it made
But not on earth its always the same –
Well a new bints fresh but only in name.

Lets break their self destroying role
Of useless loves without a goal
Whether shes virgin whether shes whore
I cant get fulfilment – not evermore.
Either its her or maybe its me
Whose the exploited we'll never agree –
Pathetic she lies on her back with her fag
May be that it – I try a new drag
And ride on a star – the trip of my life
Wow now we're away and leaving the strife.
Boy fabulous here to weave in the air
Weightless seeing her beauty so fair
A sense of fulfillment but only for now
The walls are so heavy they're crushing us now
I surface, I gasp, cry out for a breath
I'm shaking and stricken and staring at death
Still lacking the weed has no thrill anymore
How was it Blake had the vision he saw
I'll try for a fix
Mutual indulgence –
Its only for kicks!
My self is still sadder
I yearn for repose
And crave some purpose
In being, God knows.

This trip will be best
I'm off on my tod ....
The box is packing music
And the pitch is mighty fine
I see the people of the world
Upon its muddy face
And these that love like I have done

Are lost without a trace
But those who offer first themselves
With dignity find love –
The other sod's a person –
Not an object without face
A soul that yearns for being
And a heart in search of grace
Yep, I see most all the people
In the self same noose as me
Their relationships exploit them
And expose them to frustration
in the vort of misery.

Now the fix is nearly ended
And the visions fading fast
I hear the Angels singing
Is this heaven itself at last?
The walls stretch into darkness
And they run with blood so red
He says its poppy peta

Who's this voice from out the dead
It all sounds strange but magic
And the trumpet thrills my veins
He says they've solemn faces
And the medals flash with light
Again there comes the vision
Of a heavenly angel bright
Is this winged Angel death
Or Victor in the mud of Mons
Did they who live and they who died,
Find peace in service side by side –
Like a tide of restless faces, They sing
The organ peels again
A strange triumphant hymn
Their faces hold fulfillment
Of valiant heart they sing.

Now the squares and rounds dissolve
In trembling sweat I live
I see with new born eyes
The love that satisfies
They gave themselves
The essence of the God made man
To give not get my life must be
To find the love that sets me free.

11.11.1964

Appendix 2: Poems of my Life

The Canvas

How fresh art thou, clad in green,
Who wanders on this rural scene;
Who paintest all this pleasant land
With brush so gentle, so gentle hand ...
Who breathes on it the breath of life
And setest all this place of strife
Alive! With many a bell
Or dainty foxglove in the dell.
The hedgerows burst with leafy flower,
And winter goes into her bower
For she doth fear this artisan
Whose work is praised by every man;
And whom the golden sun allies
To clear white winter from the skies.
Whose furtive fingers work unseen
Preparing vista's new and green;
Until with many parting tears
Spring leaves us as in bygone years.

Whilst as those tears refresh the earth
This land makes ready to give birth
To yet a more enhancing child
Whose hair is gold, and rather wild;
Who like a mighty enfilade,
Makes the green of cornfields fade
To now display in its ephemeral life
A field of golden glory – for the knife!
Oh virile child of Summertime
Heated devil of the pantomime,
Thou has burnt the very air
And mocked old winter in her lair;

But thy beast is yet too sure
For thou has now as ever more
Been overwhelming in thy heat
And none but thine own self doth cheat.

So now the wind with talons strong
Grasps the leaves as it stalks along
And mocks the trees so bold, yet bare
Which as a tonsured monk stand there
Defying still the hoary blast
Who on them scorning shrieking case
A force of elemental storm
Displayed in crafty cryptic form.
Though even still destruction bent
On autumn's task imperial sent;
You have that grain of good sown there
That even mortals seem to share;
And in titanic apparent rage
You leave behind the storm, you wage,
A field of gold strews in the wood
Where many may see that "God is good".

Bulbarrow Hill
March 1946

To the Sky

Inestimal beauty
Starry delight
Blue of the soul
My eyes alight
Tell of wonder
Oh exquisite eve,
Show to the world
The heavens believe
Enhancing and matchless
No canvas could touch
The immeasurable greatness
Of one who made such
Omnipotent reigning
Commanding the void
Nebulous glory
Of whiteness and froid,
Unhanded by men
Who puny and weak
Such incalculable wonder
Could never compete
Virginal other
Ordained unconquerable
Show us thy Maker
Almightily honourable;
King in the Highest
Designer Divine
Intangible hands
Inconceivably fine
Pearls in the carpet
Of regalist blues

Diamonds flashing
With countless hues,
Diaphanous clouds
Crossing the sky
Ethereal exuberance
Amazing the eye ....
Thine be the Glory
And Thine be the Praise,
Lauding eternal
To Thy Name we raise.

May 1946

The Moon's Secret

As She gathered her skirts of light and left
Having danced all day in a golden dress
The last red ray swept away from the floor
And Night took her place in a sequined gown.
How gracious; gliding, she crosses the sea
Where a path of silver, shimmering light
Lies stretching far 'neath the alluring sky;
As over the mountains she dares to rise
Her dress cut low to show her creamy skin
Which, with enchanting beauty, holds spellbound
The very pulse of him who loves the day.
Her long black tresses on her shoulders lie,
Her face is radiance, sister to the day.
Her look is cold yet some refreshment brings
To tired souls who labour'd with the sun.
Is she not wondrous in her beauty, say,
Her form 'neath tulle sequined gown, so bold.
Those sequins shooting sparkling crystal darts
Lo, are they not numberless as the stars?
Her gown and hair, so black, ist as the Night?
And see her skirts fly wide and high about her,
As measureless as the mighty heavens?
Come, pray hold me not nescient of her name
'Tis not fair to belie me further.   Stay,
Draw not a nebulous net before me
Let's hear her name, who owns the dress, the night,
For dalliance is her task, oh beauty bright!
'Oh damsel, mistress of mine, your name .....'
She answered not a word but danced away.

July 1946

Soliloquy on Truleigh Hill

Swish slips the grass by my trousers
Crunch crack the twigs 'neath my feet
I stride swiftly onward and upward
Enjoying the golden heat.
The air is clear ...
So fresh up here ...
And nature near ...
How I love the drowsy heat.

In silent stillness snowswept slopes
Lonely as land could be
I was there with downcast hopes
Just the Downs alone with me.
In the Sun's pale glow
Which scarce can show
The shimmering snow
I stood with ice cold feet.

Squawk! ... A flutter of wings!
A bird flies up from the ground ...
And stay –
A nest I've found
As I walked with my eyes asleep ...
How conscious of life I feel,
Its trials, its love, and its hate,
Of its tenderness too –
As I stare at the nest
Her achievement – those gems of blue.
Above the skylark hovers in the air
To sing his poets song.

There are crickets chirping in the grass
To help the world along
This day when the Prince is Spring
It's so good to be alive; ...
But, out to sea, a cloud appears
And rain will rail the Prince ...
Yet, another Spring will reign next year
And He will be just as young.

May 1947

For "Her"

Is not the glorious beauty of this radiant spring
A song with which our hearts should sing
Yet how, when many a pace
Lies there between you and this place,
How canst thou sing with me?

As dusk draws down her curtain o'er the fading day
And ont its velvet blue her stars display
I see Orion, hunter of the night,
Shining as tho' to put the moon to flight;
Look! You can see through window panes, the night as I,
The moon that doth upon the tree tops lie
Who casts her gentle garments in your room
Upon your bed the silent silver moonbeams strewn;
So over me, my face, and down the silent trees
She casts the self-same mantle with each case
That we, beneath that cloak, though far apart
Are close; reflected in her face ... your eyes, your heart.

The bluebells droop their heads and slumber 'neath the sky
The wood sleeps to the soft winds sigh
So I my bed must find,
And close the casements of my mind
To see you in my dreams –

May 1947

The Test Match Lament

In the hours of the Test
Hulton's thirty was our best
This may stir our Grace's rest
    Sweet Spirit comfort him.

Fifty two a meagre score
Rather made the papers sore
"How", they said "the coaches swore!"
    Sweet Spirit comfort them.

Win the toss – Invent the game!
Then to prove our 'sporting name'
Let the Aussies take the fame –
    Sweet Spirit comfort us.

(Apologies to Robert Herrick – tho' I can't think why!)
    Oval 1948

The Passage of the Years

With hurrying hand at chiming bell
Men mark the passage of the years,
And yet by these how can I tell
The joy prevailing thro' the tears?

If I but of your Thought could take a cup
And say "thus many times 'twas lifted up!"
I should your love to me have failed to show
For how could I account thy giving so?

Or, would that I could truly make
Reflected here in what you see,
The best which from yourselves you take
And freely offer unto me:

For, by an image such as this I'd show
(Whilst still confessing this the debt I owe)
What debt is here which never could be paid
Though honoured in, that it was ever made.

Therefore to you I pen this line
That: though imperfect it may be,
Yet shall you recognise the sign
Of gratitude expressed by me.

September 1949

Johnian Thoughts

How oft to these remembered walls
Have turned my waking thoughts, as falls
My step upon this well worn stone
That alma mater calls me home
To where I at sweet learnings breast
Have all my ignorance confessed.

Here stood in this familiar Court
And savoured of its secret thought
As I with your remembered sons
Well known and countless lesser ones
In Hall have read the grace before
Their few brief terms too quickly fly
As wind upon the Backs doth sigh
And gowned like I they wander by

Here as with Nash I saw the moon
Upon these Courts, her silver strewn
That cool and silent star stud sky
Wherein the aged secrets lie
And now as then despite the night
From many sets stream chinks of light.

Cambridge 1950

Saint Valentine's Day

Dearest, on my darling, were ever eyes so bright
Were ever lips so red, or skin so soft and white?
Was ever such a task to write of beauty rare,
To paint with wordy brush, a loveliness so fair?
Yet, you, before my eyes, these present moments show
Such beauty as no man has dared to dream to know.
So, trying not thy beauty to this page confine
I can but simply say to you "Will you be mine"
- Because – I love you so ......

February 1950

Of "You and "I"

When shall this bloom yet blossom still more fair,
Or can this heart, too full, yet fuller be?
Can you, your face, your form, your fetching hair,
More lovely be the more of it I see?
Together, touching, can we closer be
And imitate the waves in their embrace;
Eternal, rising, surging as the sea,
Displaying strength; and gentle Beauty's face
When moonlit waves caress the quiet night:
Thus do we live, and treading virgin ways
Find yet still deeper depths and higher heights
In which our hearts may move throughout the days;
So greater joys for us shall still arise,
Since viewing each, we see though lovers' eyes.

April 1950

"Introversion" or "Conscience"!

How now, the gods have made a merry state'
For, with their blund'ring hand, which we call fate,
He that should thus their genius be
Must we call mad. For there we see
In him that should their wisdom show,
By his own mind, in argument to know
Between himself his mind divide,
And having fought in fight for either side,
Decree that by this twin cleaved brain
His 'inspiration', that's its name!
Is such that we who live in normal life
Know not the wisdom founded in such strife.
Thus, when we fondly say; "He is
But mad who eats his heart away
On problems of gargantuan size."
We know, that all the world is lies,
Since he who tears the mind he owns
Is not to madness gone;
But they who think it so.

April 1951

226

Of Love, or Retrospection

With bow bent full, that loosed shaft flow deep
Into the heart and mind that once was mine;
That heart is now for Thee, my pulses leap,
My mind no knowing has, save that for Thine.

Yet, shuttered from the world with whom I dwelt,
I anchored in the bay that was your Love
Plumbed deeper depths and sharper senses felt
Than dreamt I, in this world, a man could prove.

Yet, such is love; to know the hills of bliss,
Fond parting's tears, the new togetherness.
The upturned lip, the measure of our kiss,
The strength of life, the strange deep tenderness.

But then the paradox of love finds rest
In the etern'ty of Her lover's breast.

September 1951

London

Strange City of two thousand years
Who draws in mighty merchants trade,
How close the far-off shore appears
When , in thy breast, her wealth is made
The festive sport of tycoons play,
Who hold life's business to the glass
Make Business, Life and Work away
Whilst Beauty's sands too quietly pass.
What, though I know, from in Thy stones
A Kingdom's heart finds power to beat,
Yet from Thy stomach comes the moans
Of human brains, digested, meat
Crushed on Thy molar desks by day,
Then spewed out at night, along
The subterranean, swaying way
All jostling in the swirling throng,
And choking with Thy smoky breath
They flee the watchman's lamp before
And hurry home to Life, or Death,
Love, Hate or Pain within their door ...
"Proud City, where's Thy shame tonight?"
Is it that bright and lurid light
Cloaked o'er the stones which Thou dost own;
Amid the stars of each man's home?

October 1951

Of Time's Duplicity

Our flower blossomed for one year
Then you, with partings sharp swift blade
Have sever'd that which was most dear,
And set aside the vows we made.

Distracted, and in foolish heart,
With memory's dew this twelve month past
In blossom rare, and kept apart,
This hothouse bloom was made to last.

But, as all flowers, it has died –
Though not forgotten, yet, unmourned.

July 1952

The Cruise

Though mine, I sail a wanton vagrant yacht
Who pulls so hard the hands that check her sheets
Or heels, so to the strong winds eye she beats
And chuckling onto crested wavelets top.

At night, she rides the shimm'ring murky deep
Her mast probing excited starry space;
Her decks, all dewy, hold the pale moon's face
And, restlessly, she rocks our dreams to sleep.

Yet mine, she carries one I would were mine,
For here we slept so close, but did not touch
We were so near, and yet, our hearts as such
Did never love, and do not now entwine.

Norfolk
September 1952

The Seagull

See here the sun breaks though the misty morn
And Thames' breath subdues the man made scene
A steely forest, derricks, cranes, forlorn
Which by the moving murky waters lean.

Here massive buildings crowd the muddy shore
And on the backcloth, faint, ethereal drawn
The Tower, reflects as in Time's mirror'd door
A warning to the Bridge's slothful yawn.

And here, across the spanning bridge, you see
A myriad of your makers, chained to you
Who move beneath that Seagull, flying free
And see in him, their souls fly free and true.

So, swooping, soaring, cleaving through the air,
"Finds your white body joy, and freedom, there?"

London Bridge
December 1952

Whilst returning Home

The feathery fingers finely traced
     Against the redd'ning West,
       The spacious blue,
       Of the sunset's rays
And the shades, as the day seeks rest.

A crystal star in the high deep sky
     Calls on the faithless moon
       The sharp black house
       And the lazy smoke
Fade, in my sight, too soon.

The soft wet turf and the warm south wind
     Together give new life
       My heart awakes
       And my soul
Is touched, after the City's strife.

Chipstead Golf Course
February 1953

The Voyage

We seek not what we know
But striving still
Our questing souls pursue a chartless way;
Across unending seas
We move
And turn not back.

Surely sweet muse can tell
Or prophet point my way –
Ambition be my goad or guide
Or gentleness, or grace
Redeem my day.

Yet seek a kingdom here?
Or plan a guileless home?
Stay, watch the others on their way
Or seek a secret cell,
Find lowliness or fame
But find, and know, the way ....

Ah! There's perplexity
For who can say (for me)
The Here, or Now
Or be the light on which to point ambition's prow.

And yet the hands of older men can point
Or be upheld;
And I can sup upon sweet learning's milk, and know:
Yet greater freshment can I find
For out religious jagged rock, can flow
A healing water and the peace of mind:
Besides, dear hands can seek for mine
And loving eyes
Say all the man can need to know.

1954

Gibraltar

With in our home
May hearts enfold
And in Gibraltar peace
Forever hold
The love that I renew this day
Which is for you and is for aye
Bright in sweet Sussex shine
A beacon for our children and our time,

Gibraltar Farm
Firle, Sussex
11th October 1958 - 1979

Ladies Livery

As Aphros from the sea was made
From petalled bosom's blue brocade
Rise perfect (as you cast your cape)
'Your creamy shoulders' lovely shape;
And so you glide with measured tread
Still, vainly do, your roses red
Outbid the beauty given you
Of lips as fresh as morning dew –
Here round us marble maidens stand
In Drapers; Hall, neath painters' hand
Unsmiling canvas kings look down
And wish away the royal crown ...
To live, on this especial day
When you to Beauty's self display
A manifest, of all their dreams ....
    .... And mine -

Drapers' Hall
1959

Peterbu – Danebu

Oh silent world we hear you
Quietness in the evening time
And here hot noon day sun
Is cold beside the fire bright pine

In lake of liquid freshness here we bathe
The cool cleanness of its fresh dark depths
The languid drooping fir trees wave
As on the mountain face we climb.

Peace rippled by the trout plucked flies
From evenings warm south western breeze
A cow bell echoes through the trees
And in the summer stillness no bird cries.

Darkness if not a part
Of this light midnight world
Were watchful mornings summer light
Shines over Norway's ridged and vallied heart.

Sweet other worldliness of Summer here
Where all the rocks prepare for snow
The deep and winter solitude
Which even here in summer is the gift of Peterbu.

Aurdal Norway
1970

The Fortunate Isles

White flecked the waves from Tean
Licks across the bay
Soaring like Easter gulls
On this all joyous day –
Man's soft green turf slopes gently down
Beneath the heathers wastes to old church town
The glorious sun that pierces sharp tongued wind.
Down smugglers path, on past the school
From Grimsbys o'er the hill
Down meadow land and past the golden gorse
The people come to sing for joy
The isles of peace and liberty galore
Gives Love and Peace and Awe.

Easter Day (JJ Birthday)
Tresco 1974
Isles of Scilly

The Electronic Age

We with the science of the years
Distill sweet knowledge
For the forward way
And rearrange the moments to find forms
A binal pulse stores knowledge
In lectronic brains
And thermal nuclear alterations give us power
But all we have is change
Though not one neutron have we gained
The metamorphous of our sphere
Is known as "wisdom" and energy unleashed for strength
What gain have we in charity or love.

The City desk
London 1982

Time Past

Time past needs not this written line –
For here tomorrow lies asleep, and may be
For future's not alone the day determined
But the gift of Fortune's wheel.

Alone 'the day that was' in mine to hold
and not forget.
Or cast aside into the sea of 'not-to-be
remembered' past
So as the swan from out the gloom
of murky rivers drabness
Whiteness and beauty come unsought.

There needs no memory's cell to hold –
For fast upon the living self remains
The days remembered.

Those eyes that hold the joy of spring
and laughing,
Keep in check the warmth of Summer's Sun
The self that swan like is both strong and soft
of regal bearing and a homeliness.

A daughter, proud and yet a loving child at heart
Ah, there's the clue –
In all uncertain life the present and the past is yours
The future yet to take.

No man can say for you
Nor Priest or Parent guide that choice
Alone to each decide ......   if this be Love.

Are these the dreams that are more real
The more of them we see?
Or do they turn to dust and crumble with the break of day?
Are we .... but that's for you to say
The truth like love is hard to know
And if we seek too hard it may be lost
For happiness is given never found –

Firle 1984

Vasiliko at Dawn

Was ever world so still
Clouds in seas at dawn
Ripples twist, and clearly seen
Rusty anchors in tiny forest of kelp
The minnows in their secret world
Hurrying they only know to where
Orange and blue the caiques sleeps on
Their props of trees. White hulled
She sorts the yellow nets;
With grey and black of youth, generations all
The family together unravelling the tangle of timelessness
And one more day so many others
But one new precious moment of time like no other
Never repeated yet constant
Continuing begins this happening of stillness.

Greece 1985

The Children's Hope

The psychiatric cry is love the young
For this gives balance to the mind?
So we must first be wraught in them
Then for their world
An equanimity we find
No man can hold eternal life
We cannot save from fire or sword
Yet giving love, we give the strength beyond ourselves
To hold our sons, when we are gone
To lift them up unto the Sun.

Firle 1986

Kornate Archipelago

Jadron so deep so blue
Show us the pearl we seek of you
As swiftly on your moving face
Appears our creamy wake
And far behind
Long lines the endless repetition make
Hot sun and clearness here
Brown skin to greet the wanderer.

Yugoslavia 1986

A Downland Idyll

Out of the swirling galaxies of gasses moving but immovable in the mists of time I am part of immortality the spark of the infinite an all seeing eye of the all seen and I yearn to know those who live, albeit temporarily, outside this constance space in the confines of time itself.

The energy that is the Creator that is beauty, truth and strength combined knows all, sees all, understands all but with infinite gentleness and compassion hopes for the redemption of all those locked outside of immortality.

I must go for you and see for myself, I must dive as a hawk seeing both the great expanse and yet picking out the tiniest shrew running between the standing corn.

I will focus from that realm which needs no focus down into time itself and see how those enslaved by its moving hands have understood anything of that immortality which is to be or simply laboured for that hour which exists.

Hurtling through that impossible barrier which is time itself on which is rent only by what mortals call death, my hurtling vision focused on a thousand years which are as nothing but I saws in them a Downland Sanctuary and from it came yearnings of immortality over all the hours and days of those thousand years.

Praise was given to the Creator who is forever, favour beseeched, promises made, and confessions unburdened.

Surely in that brief span and in the still briefer lives that are the seconds of the minutes and the minutes that are the years of the hour that are the century's I saw joy and happiness all that is good and beautiful and I saw sadness for of that is mortality made and not the infinite love of the infinite truth that is of all time.

I am a traveller in time and I see a sanctuary that strives to be beyond time and the sanctuary is a people and within people and it is here as I see the hidden green waves on the Sussex downs.

Firle 1989

Firle Beacon

The blush of dawn suffused the night clouds frown
As gentle morn came rolling o're the downs
As soft as wavelets on the mornings shore
And earth was yet more lovely then before.

Ascension Day 1998

A Birthday Thought

Marked down the ages
Stand the monuments of men
Faint aspiration to an immortality
Within the changing years
We have no need of Mecca
Or the pharaohs sphinx
There is no scared spot
Save in the heart
No proof by things or gifts
Only the knowledge that is true
And truth is now
And of all time.

Of what is past remember hours of ease
Lights rippling on the mirrored waters darkened face
A country walk when spring gave freshness to the air
And then the age old inn when twilight burnished sun has reddened
all the sky.

These hours and a host beside
Gay laughter and the chink of glass
Within the social whirl
Or when the hooves were thudding on the turf
External moments when an organ breathed Bach's magic in the air.

Firle
September 2003

Printed in Great Britain
by Amazon